A Cloud of Witnesses

"This is a compelling story—researched carefully, narrated clearly, and interpreted contextually. The history of Indonesia's three Anabaptist-Mennonite synods serves to introduce the 17th global assembly of the Mennonite World Conference, scheduled to convene in Semarang, Indonesia, in July 2022. Even more, the book provides an Anabaptist-Mennonite perspective on the great transformation in world Christianity that has occurred in recent decades, with special insight concerning missionary activity, indigenous evangelization, colonial paternalism, revivals, violent civil disorder, charismatic gifts, agricultural education, internal church disagreements, miracles, relations with Islam, megachurches, and more."

—**MARK NOLL**, historian and coauthor of *Clouds of Witnesses:*
  Christian Voices from Africa and Asia

"*A Cloud of Witnesses* is a rich, informative, crunchy, and tasty glimpse into Indonesian Anabaptist-Mennonite churches—GITJ, GKMI, JKI—written in a broader Anabaptist-Mennonite history by a proven historian, John D. Roth himself. This book is written with a passion for and dedication to Christ and reflects a commitment to the global Anabaptist family through Mennonite World Conference. Grab a copy, and I will see you in Indonesia! Congratulations, Pak John!"

—**REV. ANDIOS SANTOSO**, former general secretary of GKMI
  (2014–19) and member of the Mission Commission of MWC

"This fascinating study shows why Mennonites should embrace their identity as a multicultural faith community. I recommend it very highly, both for the story it tells of Mennonites in Indonesia and for the valuable insights it contains for Christian communities around the world."

—**DANA L. ROBERT**, Truman Collins professor of World Christianity and History of Mission at Boston University School of Theology and author of *Christian Mission: How Christianity Became a World Religion*

"An excellent travel guide for all people who will attend the forthcoming Mennonite World Conference assembly in Semarang in 2022. In a lucid style, John Roth provides a concise historical and socioreligious context of Indonesia and a clear picture of the origins of the three Mennonite conferences in this vast, hospitable country and their present situation with the challenges they face. Those readers who will follow the assembly at home are not only given a perfect handbook, but can even taste the spirit of the assembly by trying the recipes in the final section of the book. Selamat menikmati bacaan bagus ini! (Enjoy reading this nice book!)"

—**ALLE G. HOEKEMA**, retired associate professor of theology at the Free University Amsterdam

"This book successfully describes the Mennonite community in Indonesia that grew up in three different conferences, each of which has a unique culture and background. It tells us not only about the past, but also about struggles in the current Indonesian context. This book helps readers 'taste' the flavor of Mennonites in Indonesia."

—**DANANG KRISTIAWAN**, Javanese Mennonite Church (GITJ) Jepara/Wiyata Wacana Seminary in Pati, Indonesia

A Cloud of Witnesses

Celebrating
Indonesian Mennonites

John D. Roth

HERALD
P R E S S

Harrisonburg, Virginia

Herald Press
PO Box 866, Harrisonburg, Virginia 22803
www.HeraldPress.com

Library of Congress Cataloging-in-Publication Data
Names: Roth, John D., 1960- author.
Title: A cloud of witnesses: celebrating Indonesian Mennonites / John D. Roth.
Description: Harrisonburg, Virginia : Herald Press, 2021. | Includes
    bibliographical references.
Identifiers: LCCN 2021016318 (print) | LCCN 2021016319 (ebook) | ISBN
    9781513809397 (paperback) | ISBN 9781513809403 (epub)
Subjects: LCSH: Mennonites—Indonesia. | Indonesia—Church history.
Classification: LCC BX8119.I5 R68 2021 (print) | LCC BX8119.I5 (ebook) |
    DDC 289.7/598—dc23
LC record available at https://lccn.loc.gov/2021016318
LC ebook record available at https://lccn.loc.gov/2021016319

Study guides are available for many Herald Press titles at
www.HeraldPress.com.

A CLOUD OF WITNESSES
© 2021 by Herald Press, Harrisonburg, Virginia 22803. 800-245-7894.
    All rights reserved.
Library of Congress Control Number: 2021016318
International Standard Book Number: 978-1-5138-0939-7 (paperback);
    978-1-5138-0940-3 (ebook)
Printed in United States of America
Cover photo by Amy Gingerich
Cover and interior design by Merrill Miller

Unless otherwise noted, Scripture text is quoted, with permission, from the *New
Revised Standard Version*, © 1989, Division of Christian Education of the National
Council of Churches of Christ in the United States of America.

25 24 23 22 21   10 9 8 7 6 5 4 3 2 1

Contents

Foreword 7

Map 10

1 The Emergence of a Global Anabaptist-Mennonite
Church 11

2 An Introduction to Indonesia 35

3 Before Pieter Jansz There Was Tunggul Wulung:
The Early History of the Javanese Mennonite Church . . 55

4 The Evangelical Javanese Church
(Gereja Injili di Tanah Jawa—GITJ) 81

5 The Muria Christian Church of Indonesia
(Gereja Kristen Muria Indonesia—GKMI) 107

6 The Indonesian Christian Congregation
(Jemaat Kristen Indonesia—JKI) 133

7 The Indonesian MWC Churches Today 155

A (Very Brief!) Travel Guide to Indonesia 167

Recipes to Try at Home 183

The Author 199

Foreword

*I*LOVE CHRISTIAN MOSAICS. Mosaics are fascinating art-
work. Traditionally, mosaics are made by organizing dozens
of small stones together in a specific way. When you focus your
attention on a few of them, you can note that some are irregu-
lar while others are smooth. Depending on your point of view,
some stones may be considered relatively standard, while others
may be treasurable. However, that is not the point of a mosaic.
To get its message, you need to take distance from the piece of
art and get a general view of it. In that way, you will see how
each small stone is in a place that, along with the others, ends
up creating a larger, unified image. Mosaics transmit a message
through the sum of their many parts, not the individual pieces.

It is not a coincidence that mosaics have been used in
churches throughout history. Our global church is itself like a
mosaic. All of us, together, transmit or present a unified image
to the world. We hope that image is Jesus' image. That is, at
least, our call. Such an image requires a view of the whole body

and not just a focus on a small piece of our global community of faith. Seeing only one church in one geographical place, or even a church in a brief historical period, does not give us a complete picture of Jesus. We need to find distance to see how all the pieces fit together and perceive a fuller image of Jesus.

In this delightful book, John Roth helps us do precisely that. He offers us a general view of Indonesia's church, its history, culture, and current challenges to point us toward an important message. Such a message will be lost if we pay attention to only one period of its history or focus our attention on only one segment of the Anabaptist church in that country. But why Indonesia?

In the words of John Roth, the Anabaptist church in Indonesia offers a superb introduction to the Anabaptist global movement. Being the oldest Mennonite community outside Europe and North America, it brings together different experiences distributed in several churches worldwide.

In our Anabaptist community, some churches find themselves in contexts of persecution, while others enjoy freedom and prosperity. Some of our members face challenges because of the patterns of financial dependency. Others deal with church conflicts and divisions. There are churches with a strong evangelistic focus, and some have a long experience in social and development ministries. Some churches copy Western worship styles (traditional or charismatic), while others look for indigenous liturgy and theology.

In our global family, you can find models of authoritarian leadership and models of egalitarian organization. Some churches grow by absorbing existing congregations, while others evangelize and send missionaries to other cultures. Some churches emerged as intentional agrarian communities, while others flourish in urban settings. Some have solid mission, education, health, and service institutions, while others struggle with patterns of paternalism and complex relations with foreign Mennonite agencies.

Some of our members develop their call amid persecution, nationalism, racism, revolution, and war. Others are a minority in their encounter with other faiths. Many churches have integrated Anabaptist values with a Pentecostal understanding of their faith.

You can find all these characteristics and many more in the history and present of the church of Indonesia. It is a microcosm of our global community, a small mosaic that introduces a bigger picture. With Roth's expert guidance, I trust you will receive the message of this church's mosaic. His broader knowledge of the worldwide Anabaptist church, mixed with his theological insights and history training, introduces us to one fascinating Christian church: a church that, by its history and present, conflicts and reconciliation, challenges and achievements, shows the image of Jesus to the world.

—*César García*
General Secretary of Mennonite
World Conference

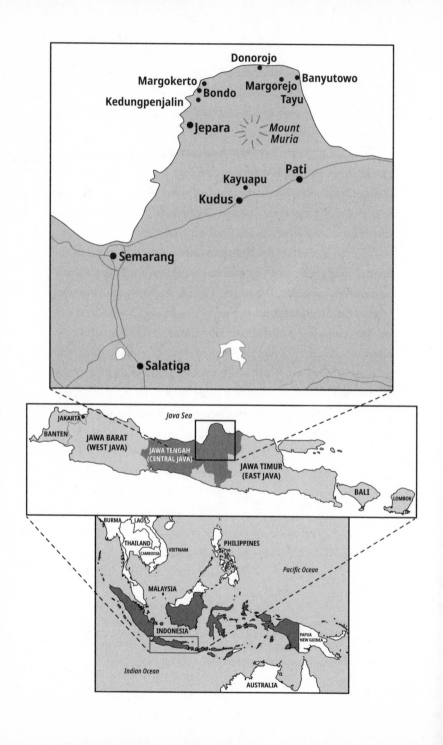

1

The Emergence of a Global Anabaptist-Mennonite Church

*O*N AUGUST 10, 1952, Tan King Ien, leader of the Chinese Mennonite churches in Java, Indonesia, greeted an audience of twelve hundred people who had gathered for worship just outside Basel, Switzerland, as part of the fifth global assembly of the Mennonite World Conference (MWC). "The fact that I can stand before you this morning," he said through a translator,

> is evidence that this conference is made up of people from
> different races, with different languages and customs.
> Nevertheless, it feels to me as if we are one family. It is the
> strong and loving hand of the Lord that has brought us here
> and binds us together. Only through that love can we feel as
> one—one in baptism, one in faith, and one in the Savior.[1]

---

1. H. S. Bender, Liesel Widmer, and Paul Schowalter, eds. *Die Gemeinde Christi und Ihr Auftrag: Vorträge und Verhandlungen der Fünften Mennonitischen Weltkonferenz vom 10. bis 15. August 1952, St. Chrischona bei Basel, Schweiz* (Karlsruhe, Germany: Heinrich Schneider, 1953), 34.

Tan King Ien's words to the assembly—supplemented the following day by a greeting from Soehadiweko Djojodihardjo, chair of the Javanese Mennonite synod—marked the first occasion in which anyone from Asia had participated in a gathering of the Mennonite World Conference. Indeed, according to historian Alfred Neufeld, "It was probably the first time that representatives of the Mennonite churches in the global North were asked to listen to the pilgrimage of a new member in a public gathering speaking in a completely foreign language."[2]

Although MWC regarded itself as a global body, in reality the 214 delegates who attended the gathering in 1952 represented only six countries—all from Europe and North America.[3] Shortly after the Indonesian leaders spoke, Harold S. Bender, MWC chair, summarized the composition of the global Anabaptist-Mennonite fellowship.[4] According to his estimates, the Anabaptist-Mennonite family comprised 300,000 baptized members, with 200,000 living in North America and another 70,000 in western Europe and the Soviet Union. This left approximately 30,000 baptized members—or 10 percent—in the "mission fields of the East Indies, India, China, Tanzania, Congo, Argentina, and Puerto Rico."[5]

---

2. Alfred Neufeld, *Becoming a World Communion: Theological Developments in Mennonite World Conference from 1925 to 1975* (Asunción, Paraguay: Universidad Evangélica, 2018), 166.

3. In addition to the two visitors from Indonesia, three guests from South America were also present at the assembly.

4. "Anabaptist-Mennonite" is a general term intended to include all those groups who trace their origin to the Radical Reformation of the sixteenth century, and continue to practice adult, or believers, baptism. It is an umbrella category that includes numerous branches of Mennonites, Amish, and Hutterites, and, in the MWC context, the Brethren in Christ.

5. *Die Gemeinde Christi und Ihr Auftrag*, 70–71.

Twenty-five years later, when the tenth global assembly of MWC convened in Wichita, Kansas, the composition of the global Anabaptist-Mennonite church had changed dramatically. In 1978, participants in the gathering were welcomed by MWC's president, Million Belete, a dynamic leader of the Meserete Kristos Church in Ethiopia.[6] Over the next five days, worship services featured sermons or extended testimonies from Venancio Gonzales (Paraguay), Mayambi Diakande (Zaire), Albert Widjaja (Indonesia), Festo Kivengere (Uganda), and Takashi Yamada (Japan). Respondents to various presentations included Charles Christano (Indonesia), Kedi Delchume (Ethiopia), Felonito Sacapaño (Philippines), Alvaro Fernandez (Uruguay), Michio Ohno (Japan), Dick Ekerete (Nigeria), Luis Correa (Colombia), and Kilabi Bululu (Zaire [Democratic Republic of Congo]). The assembly featured choirs from Taiwan, India, and Kenya, and concluded with the election of Charles Christano (Indonesia) as MWC's president, and the appointment of vice presidents from Africa, Asia, and Central and South America to serve alongside those from Europe and North America.

Clearly, something significant had shifted in the global Anabaptist-Mennonite church between 1952 and 1978. By 1978, the Anabaptist family had doubled in size to include 610,000 baptized members—with 315,000 in North America and 95,000 in Europe and the Soviet Union. More telling was the fact that churches in Asia, Africa, and Latin America now accounted for an estimated 200,000 members, or one-third of the total.

---

6. Paul N. Kraybill, ed., *The Kingdom of God in a Changing World: Proceedings of the Tenth Assembly, Mennonite World Conference, Wichita, Kansas, July 25–30, 1978* (Lombard, IL: Mennonite World Conference, 1979).

In the years since then, the shift in the church's center of gravity from North to South—a transformation that scholars such as David Barrett, Philip Jenkins, and Lamin Sanneh have insightfully documented for the larger Christian church as well—has continued at a remarkable pace.[7] In 2018, Mennonite World Conference identified slightly more than 2.1 million baptized Anabaptist-Mennonites in the world, of whom approximately 1.5 million were members of MWC churches.[8] Among MWC member groups, only 19 percent lived in Europe or North America, with 49 percent from Africa, 25 percent from Asia, and 7 percent from Latin America. Put differently, today 81 percent of MWC members reside in what is often called the "global South." According to the Institute for the Study of Global Anabaptism, 93 percent of all baptisms in the global Anabaptist-Mennonite church since 2001 have occurred outside Europe or North America.[9] Today, the largest national church body among MWC members is the Meserete Kristos Church of Ethiopia, with nearly 400,000 baptized members, followed by churches in India and the Democratic Republic of Congo. To frame it in still another way, in 2018 the *combined* membership of Mennonite Church USA and

7. The literature on global Christianity is vast and growing rapidly. For a basic introduction, see Philip Jenkins, *The Next Christendom: The Coming of Global Christianity* (Oxford: Oxford University Press, 2004), Lamin Sanneh, *Encountering the West: Christianity and the Global Cultural Process* (Maryknoll, NY: Orbis, 1993), and Mark Noll, *The New Shape of World Christianity: How American Experience Reflects Global Faith* (Downers Grove, IL: IVP Academic, 2009).

8. Cf. "Membership, Map and Statistics," Mennonite World Conference, accessed January 4, 2021, https://mwc-cmm.org/world-map-and-statistics. Those groups who are not members of Mennonite World Conference tend to be among the most traditional in terms of cultural identity—the Old Order Amish, for example, or the Hutterites, Old Colony Mennonites, and other smaller conservative groups.

9. Conrad Kanagy, Elizabeth Miller, and John D. Roth, *Global Anabaptist Profile: Belief and Practice in 24 Mennonite World Conference Churches* (Goshen, IN: Institute for the Study of Global Anabaptism, 2017), 29.

Mennonite Church Canada, along with the Mennonite Brethren and Brethren in Christ churches in North America—groups that have long considered themselves to be crucial carriers of Anabaptist identity—accounts for a mere 8 percent of the total number of Anabaptist-Mennonites in the world today.

A GLOBALIZED TRADITION

The driving forces behind this profound transformation are complex. Each group, of course, has its own story and context. But three distinct themes offer a small window into the dynamics behind the globalization of the Anabaptist-Mennonite tradition in the past seventy years.

1. Migration

One source of globalization has been the diaspora of German-speaking Mennonites, many of them fleeing their homelands as refugees of government oppression or the ravages of war. Thus, for example, in the early 1920s when provincial governments in Canada began to insist that Russian Mennonite immigrants teach their schoolchildren in English, several thousand Old Colony, or Reinländer, Mennonites immigrated to Mexico. They were followed several years later by another immigration of Sommerfelder, Bergthaler, and Chortizer Mennonites from Canada to the "Green Hell" of the Paraguayan Chaco. Thousands more fled the Bolshevik Revolution in South Russia in the late 1920s, the iron-fisted policies of Stalin in the 1930s, and the destruction of World War II in the 1940s, arriving as refugees to Paraguay and Brazil, or later to Belize, Uruguay, and Bolivia.

Today some 250,000 of these Mennonites are scattered across Mexico, Central America, and South America. The most conservative among them have established thriving colonies in isolated settings where they continue to speak a Low German dialect and maintain the religious traditions and folkways of their ancestors. The more progressive of these immigrants have settled in major cities, entered the professions, become fluent in Spanish and Portuguese, and frequently exert an economic— and sometimes political—influence far out of proportion to their numbers.

2. Missions

A second impulse behind the globalization of the Anabaptist-Mennonite tradition has been the missionary movement. Here Mennonites have followed the general trajectory of the larger history of Protestant missions, albeit with a typical time lag. The first organized Mennonite missions emerged in the Netherlands in the 1850s, soon followed by initiatives among Mennonites in South Russia. But the beginnings were very slow. Mennonites in North America had established only seven missions before 1900. Between 1900 and 1944 another eighteen mission outreaches emerged. It wasn't until the middle of the twentieth century that a new generation—shaped by their experiences in Civilian Public Service or European relief work—became much more interested in the larger world. Mennonites in the United States and Canada established more than fifty new missions in the 1950s alone and another seventy-five since then—mostly in Africa, South America, and Asia.[10]

Parallel to these missions, thousands of Mennonite young people from North America served as relief and service volunteers with Mennonite Central Committee, the Teachers Abroad

---

10. Wilbert R. Shenk, "Mission and Service and the Globalization of North American Mennonites," *Mennonite Quarterly Review* 70 (Jan. 1996): 8.

Program, PAX, or a dozen other international programs.[11] These volunteers were people with practical skills, often more inclined to offer "a cup of cold water in Christ's name" than to hold evangelistic services; but they made a profound impact on the regions where they served. Together, these international mission, service, and relief initiatives not only brought the good news of the gospel to many previously unreached regions of the world, but also embodied a distinctive expression of the Christian faith that linked conversion to a strong sense of community, a desire to follow Jesus in daily life, and a commitment to reconciliation and peacemaking, even at great personal cost. And they brought their experiences home with them.

As a result, the reality of the global Anabaptist-Mennonite church has become much more visible to local congregations in North America. Today, virtually every Mennonite congregation in the United States and Canada has some connection to the global church through a former missionary or MCC service worker, a short-term service project, a sister-church relationship, or perhaps more indirectly through the *More-with-Less Cookbook* or artisan crafts from local Ten Thousand Villages stores that have become an important decorating motif in their congregants' homes.

3. Contextualization

The real engine behind the dramatic growth in the Anabaptist-Mennonite worldwide fellowship, however, has come about through the creative efforts of leaders and laypeople in countries around the world, as recipients of the gospel retranslated the good news into their local context and made it genuinely their own.

---

11. Though fewer in numbers, European Mennonites also participated in similar mission, service, and relief initiatives.

Here, the story of the Mennonite church in Ethiopia is especially instructive. Mennonite missionaries first arrived in Ethiopia in 1945, long after other Protestant missions had already been established there. In typical fashion, they initially focused on education and healthcare, establishing elementary schools, an institute for the deaf, and several clinics and hospitals. An important shift in the character of the church began to unfold in the late 1950s, when a charismatic revival movement led to the foundation of the Meserete Kristos (Christ Is the Foundation) Church, or MKC.[12]

Political events led to another crucial transformation. When Marxist revolutionaries came to power in Ethiopia in 1974, they quickly imposed restrictions on all forms of evangelical Christianity—harassing or arresting church leaders, sometimes beating them or holding them in custody for long periods of time. Still, MKC members continued to meet. In 1982 the government officially closed the church and, for the next four years, held six of its key leaders in prison. Remarkably, however, the MKC did not die. With their leaders imprisoned and their churches shuttered, the MKC developed a new model of church life, which was strikingly Anabaptist in nature. Small cell groups, many of them led by women, met secretly in homes for prayer and Bible study. These groups quickly reorganized whenever they grew to ten or twelve participants. Leaders developed a Bible study curriculum, printed on secret presses, and required new converts to undergo an extended period of instruction and Bible study before their baptism. Above all, the

---

12. For an overview of the full MKC story, see the chapter by Alemu Checole, "Mennonite Churches in Eastern Africa," in *Anabaptist Songs in African Hearts: Global Mennonite History Series: Africa*, ed. John Allen Lapp and C. Arnold Snyder (Intercourse, PA: Good Books, 2006), 191–253.

underground church was sustained by prayer—regular sessions of intense intercession to God that often lasted for hours, and sometimes the entire night. Even though their gatherings were illegal, those who participated in the movement later recollected that "no one was afraid."[13]

The consequences were astounding. Before the period of persecution, the MKC numbered around 5,000 members. In 1991, when persecution came to an end, it had grown to a fellowship of well over 50,000 baptized members. And the growth has continued at an exponential rate ever since. Today, as noted earlier, there are nearly 400,000 baptized believers in the Meserete Kristos Church, making it the largest national Mennonite body in the world.

The central themes of the Ethiopian story have been repeated in Anabaptist-Mennonite groups in many other countries as well. As local believers have emerged in positions of leadership—and as the church has faced persecution—it has been transformed: steady growth in the churches in the Democratic Republic of Congo in the face of prolonged civil war; renewal in Zimbabwe despite a dictatorial regime and unimaginable economic hardships; and, as we shall see, a church transformed in Indonesia, often in the face of ethnic and religious persecution.

From the perspective of a five-hundred-year history, the Anabaptist-Mennonite tradition is clearly in the midst of a profound renewal and transformation.

---

13. The MKC story is recounted in Nathan B. Hege, *Beyond Our Prayers: An Amazing Half Century of Church Growth in Ethiopia, 1948–1998* (Scottdale, PA: Herald Press, 1998); as well as Brent L. Kipfer, "Thriving under Persecution: Meserete Kristos Church Leadership during the Ethiopian Revolution (1974–1991)," *Mennonite Quarterly Review* 91 (July 2017): 297–370.

WHOSE STORY?

In general, Anabaptist-Mennonites in Europe and North America—those who have traditionally understood themselves to be the standard-bearers of the tradition—have been slow to recognize this tectonic shift in the church's center of gravity and the flourishing of the Anabaptist-Mennonite tradition in seemingly strange and unfamiliar settings. Faith, of course, always takes root in a cultural context. Although the God we worship is beyond time and space, our faith finds expression in beliefs, doctrines, rituals, and forms of worship that reflect particular cultures. In principle, this is a good thing. After all, the biblical doctrine of the incarnation—the "Word made flesh"—affirms that Christ's presence in the world will always be made visible and be experienced in tangible, embodied ways.

Throughout the history of God's people, however, the enduring temptation is to regard those particular cultural expressions of faith as timeless or "essential." This has been especially true for groups in the Anabaptist-Mennonite tradition who claim a cultural heritage extending back for several generations, in which they imagine their Christian identity to be closely linked to the heroic origins of the Anabaptist movement in the sixteenth century. In this telling of the story, the Anabaptist movement endured, despite severe persecution, and continued in an uninterrupted succession as the direct descendants of the Anabaptists—now known mostly as Mennonites, Amish, and Hutterites—migrated westward to North America and eastward to Poland and to South Russia.

This sense of a shared history, sealed by persecution, reinforced an identity among many North American Mennonites as a "people set apart." The communities they formed tended to be deeply shaped by family networks, ethnic folkways, familiar worship practices, and a strong sense of historical and cultural continuity. Wherever they settled—in the steppelands of South Russia; the rich farmland of Pennsylvania, Virginia, Ohio, and Illinois; the wheatfields of Kansas; or the prairie frontier of Manitoba—Mennonites came to define themselves at least as much by their distinctive culture as by their religious convictions.

In doing so, they came perilously close to turning their particular culture into an idol—worshiping forms of their own creation rather than the living God who always exceeds human categories and definitions. Like the Pharisees of Jesus' day, contemporary Mennonites, particularly in North America, have sometimes made the preservation of familiar traditions and rituals an end in itself, rather than the means by which the living presence of God is expressed in the world. Some Mennonites in North America today, for example, find it nearly impossible to imagine Mennonite identity apart from their genealogical pedigree, historical experiences, distinctive foodways, or specific forms of worship. Indeed, some go so far as to claim that they are "Mennonite, but not Christian."[14] Such claims would sound absolutely absurd, of course, to sixteenth-century Anabaptists who forfeited their lives defending the conviction that following Christ was a conscious decision, *not* a cultural birthright.

Cultural forms of identity are further complicated by the fact that even in North America, the Anabaptist-Mennonite tradition has never been defined by a single culture, historical

---

14. Indeed, some Canadian authors have suggested that to be a "Mennonite" writer necessarily implies that you can trace your family's story back to South Russia and the culture and historical experiences that left a deep imprint on the Russian Mennonite story, thereby excising virtually the entire membership of MWC from a "Mennonite" identity.

narrative, or confession of faith. The Hutterites, for example, continue to live in colonies and practice community of goods. The Old Order Amish are visibly separated from their Mennonite neighbors by their distinctive dress and strict limitations on the use of electricity and cars. The "Russian" Mennonites who settled in the western states and provinces shared strong memories of their nineteenth-century sojourn in South Russia, including, for many, the searing experience as refugees from the Soviet Union in the early twentieth century. The Old Colony Mennonites in Mexico, Belize, Brazil, Paraguay, and Bolivia represent an entirely different set of ethnic folkways. A claim by any one of these groups to be the true embodiment of Anabaptist faith on the basis of their particular culture or tradition is both presumptuous and absurd. Why then should we be surprised or skeptical if the Anabaptist-Mennonite groups emerging in Latin America, Asia, or Africa should express their faith in cultural forms that seem very different from the Western tradition?

WHAT ARE THE BONDS THAT HOLD ANABAPTIST-MENNONITES TOGETHER?

If it is true that living traditions—attentive to the movement of the Spirit—will always be expressed in new and changing cultural contexts—how then do we recognize or name a shared sense of Anabaptist-Mennonite peoplehood? The Roman Catholic Church, with 1.1 billion members residing in virtually every country of the world, is united—at least in principle—by the authority of the pope, by the Teaching Office of the church, and by the sacrament of the mass. The 78 million members of the Lutheran Church, living in very different cultural contexts, all acknowledge the authority of the Augsburg Confession as the interpretative lens through which they read Scripture. The 80 million members of the Anglican Church do not agree with each other on many points, but they share a conviction that the spiritual authority of the priest who baptized them can be traced in an unbroken line of continuity all the way back to the apostle Peter, who received his authority to "bind and loose" from Christ himself (Matthew 16:19). Diverse Pentecostal groups around the world are united by the shared experience of "speaking in tongues" and the use of other gifts of the Spirit; and many Reformed and Baptist Christians are ready to define the unity of their churches by a specific set of unassailable theological doctrines.

In general, the Anabaptist-Mennonite tradition has not claimed *any* of these approaches as the basis for church unity. We have significant leaders, but no pope. We have confessions of faith, but no single confession or list of doctrinal beliefs that is authoritative for all groups. We share in the rituals of baptism and the Lord's Supper, but have rarely claimed these as "sacraments." Indeed, if any single person or group in the Anabaptist-Mennonite tradition would insist on naming the "essence" of our faith, other groups would almost certainly react with indignation.

So what is it that binds this particular Christian tradition together?

There is no one perfect image for describing the unity of the church. The apostle Paul used the metaphor of the body, insisting on the mutual importance and interdependency of each individual part (1 Corinthians 12). I, in turn, propose two additional images that help set the stage for this small book.

The first image is that of an atom—with a nucleus of protons and neutrons at the center, around which numerous electrons are orbiting. A recent summary of Anabaptist-Mennonite theology uses the language of "center" as a way of describing a shared point of orientation that still allows for diverse identities.[15] According to this summary of shared commitments, which has gained widespread popularity among Anabaptist-Mennonites in the global church,

1. Jesus is the center of our faith;

2. community is the center of our lives; and

3. reconciliation is the center of our work.

Though far from offering a complete theological description of the Anabaptist-Mennonite tradition, it may be useful to think of "Jesus," "community," and "reconciliation" as composing a nucleus of affirmations shared by virtually all groups in the Anabaptist-Mennonite stream of the Christian faith. At the same time, however, each of our communities is likely to claim these affirmations in different ways, expressing them with a variety of worship styles, biblical interpretations, rituals, and daily practices. Like electrons surrounding the nucleus of an atom, some will likely be closer to that common center than others. The position of each, relative to the center, will always be changing since electrons are always in motion. And some may eventually shift their orbit toward an entirely different nucleus. The image, though, is one of coherence and order (the electrons are not moving randomly), and also recognizes the inevitability of movement, interaction, and change that cannot always be controlled or predicted.

---

15. Cf. Palmer Becker, *What Is an Anabaptist Christian?* (Elkhart, IN: Mennonite Mission Network, 2008); and Palmer Becker, *Anabaptist Essentials: Ten Signs of a Unique Christian Faith* (Harrisonburg, VA: Herald Press, 2017).

A second image for describing the relationship of Anabaptist-Mennonite groups is the botanical metaphor of a rhizome.[16] Rhizomes are underground plant stems that propagate by sending out a profusion of roots laterally horizontal to the soil above. The rhizome's interconnected roots develop nodes that send sprouts up above the ground, which appear in unexpected places. These sprouts appear to be distinct entities. But under the soil, they are joined together in a complex web of horizontal relationships. Rhubarb, lilies, bamboo, and aspen trees are all rhizomes. Indeed, the Pando colony of aspens in Utah consists of nearly fifty thousand trees extending over one hundred acres that is a single living organism. Studies have found that trees in the colony "sense" damage done to trees in another part of the grove, even those at a far distance.[17]

A rhizome, write social theorists Gilles Deleuze and Félix Guattari, "has no beginning or end; it is always in the middle, between things, interbeing, intermezzo."[18] As a metaphor, rhizomes suggest multiple interwoven relationships of connectivity and alliances that defy easy categories. The image of the global church as a rhizome suggests that Anabaptist-Mennonite identity emerges from a complex and unpredictable constellation

---

16. Portions of the discussion here and in the next section also appear in "'Without Spot or Wrinkle': The Tendency toward Separation in the Mennonite Tradition . . . and a Vision for a 'Rhizomic' Church," in *Come Out from among Them, and Be Ye Separate, Saith the Lord: Separationism and the Believers' Church Tradition*, ed. William H. Brackney and Evan L. Colford (Cambridge, UK: Lutterworth Press, 2019), 66–82. Used with permission.

17. Cf. Michael C. Grant, "The Trembling Giant," *Discover* (Oct. 1993), available at https://www.discovermagazine.com/planet-earth/the-trembling-giant; and Ferris Jabr, "The Social Life of Forests," *New York Times*, December 2, 2020, https://www.nytimes.com/interactive/2020/12/02/magazine/tree-communication-mycorrhiza.html.

18. Gilles Deleuze and Félix Guattari, *A Thousand Plateaus: Capitalism and Schizophrenia* (New York: Continuum, 1987), 27.

of intertwining, face-to-face relationships, many of them un-planned and many happening in settings outside of academic spaces or church buildings. Such a view of the church may be frustrating to those who prefer tidy organizational charts or the linear clarity of a fixed set of doctrines. The identity of a "rhizomic" church seems risky and vulnerable—a vast web of interconnected, sometimes unpredictable, relationships whose character, like that of the Holy Spirit, is likely to always exceed our capacity to define, grasp, or pin down. But the image may also remind us that the body of Christ is the work of the Holy Spirit, which often begins as a mustard seed and bears fruit in ways that we cannot predict or control.

MENNONITE WORLD CONFERENCE: A "RHIZOMIC" ORGANIZATION

Nearly one hundred years ago, on June 13–15, 1925, a small group of Mennonite leaders—perhaps forty altogether, from seven different countries—gathered in Switzerland for several days of worship and conversation. The group hoped to rees-tablish a common sense of identity in the aftermath of World War I, a war that had brought Mennonite soldiers from France, Germany, Poland, Ukraine, and North America into mortal combat with each other. As one step to healing broken relation-ships among the groups, those present at the gathering agreed to collaborate in responding to the material and spiritual needs of the Mennonites in the Soviet Union, who had been dev-astated by the Bolshevik Revolution, along with the ensuing famine, and the subsequent imprisonment, deportation, and murder of hundreds of their members.[19]

19. *Bericht* über *die 400 jährige Jubiläums Feier der Mennoniten oder Taufgesinnten vom 13. bis 15. Juni 1925 in Basel* (Karlsruhe: Verlag Bibelheim Thomashof, 1925).

That modest gathering marked the beginning of the Mennonite World Conference.

In the years since then, representatives of various Anabaptist-Mennonite groups have continued to meet on a regular basis to hear each other's stories, to explore ways of sharing each other's burdens, and to be challenged and inspired by testimonies of Christian discipleship from many different settings.

Mennonite World Conference is—by intention and also, perhaps, a bit by accident—a rhizomic organization. In contrast to many parallel organizations in other Christian communions, its administrative footprint is very small. Its primary emphasis has not been on creating programs, but rather on strengthening relationships among its members, which today includes 107 groups. For example, the process leading to the seven "Shared Convictions"—a statement of faith embraced by Mennonite World Conference member groups in 2006—was slow and arduous, shaped by the insights of numerous churches around the world. Most publications in MWC's Global Anabaptist-Mennonite Shelf of Literature are joint projects, coauthored by writers from the global North and South.[20] The Young Anabaptist Mennonite Exchange Network (YAMEN!) volunteer program regularly links young people in the global South with service opportunities in churches elsewhere in the global South as a form of gift sharing that connects communities who would otherwise not encounter each other. The five-volume Global Mennonite History project took nearly

See also John A. Lapp and Ed Van Straten, "Mennonite World Conference 1925–2000: From Euro-American Conference to Worldwide Communion," *Mennonite Quarterly Review* 87 (Jan. 2003): 5–47.

20. A great example of this sort of collaboration is Pakisa Tshmika and Tim Lind, *Sharing Gifts in the Global Family of Faith: One Church's Experiment* (Intercourse, PA: Good Books, 2003).

fifteen years to complete, largely because the project relied heavily on local historians with a wide range of academic training, who wrote in their own languages, many of them drawing on oral sources. Most recently, in 2020, MWC served as a gathering point to coordinate more than a dozen other churches and mission agencies in the distribution of COVID-19–related relief funds to scores of Anabaptist-Mennonite churches around the world, many of whom, in turn, offered support to their local communities.

Every six years, MWC hosts a global family reunion—the global assembly—in which representatives from each of its member groups join in a General Council to discuss matters of shared concern, and visitors from all over the world gather for worship and fellowship. Recent global assemblies have been hosted in India (1997), Zimbabwe (2003), and Paraguay (2009), as well as the United States (2015), with the logistical planning borne largely by local committees of the host conferences.

In July 2022, MWC's global assembly will take place in Semarang, Indonesia, with three Indonesian church conferences—the Gereja Injili di Tanah Jawa, Gereja Kristen Muria Indonesia, and Jemaat Kristen Indonesia, or GITJ, GKMI, and JKI—serving as hosts. The history of these three groups, all members of MWC, reaches back to the middle of the nineteenth century. Indeed, they were the first Anabaptist-Mennonite churches to emerge outside of Europe and North America, with some members of the GITJ church able to trace their history with the church for six generations. An encounter with the GITJ, GKMI, and JKI churches of Indonesia is a microcosm of the contemporary global Anabaptist-Mennonite fellowship. Here we see the wonderful complexity of ethnicity, culture, faithfulness, growth, conflict, and renewal as the identity of these groups emerged over the course of the past 170 years—all dynamics which, if we are ready to pay close attention, have been part of the history of the Anabaptist-Mennonite tradition in Europe and North America as well.

GOALS OF THIS BOOK

On July 5–10, 2022, Mennonites from all around the world will gather in Semarang, Indonesia, to celebrate the 17th Assembly of Mennonite World Conference.[21] While the first MWC assembly in 1925 was attended primarily by middle-aged men, nearly all from Europe, Assembly 17 will reflect the colors, sounds, tastes, and worship styles of a church that has become truly multicultural and international. The assembly in Semarang offers a rare opportunity for participants to represent the changing face

Participants at an event in Basel, Switzerland, in 1925, celebrating the four-hundredth anniversary of the first Anabaptist baptisms in 1525. The gathering was the first meeting of what would become the Mennonite World Conference. PHOTOGRAPH COURTESY OF MENNONITE WORLD CONFERENCE

---

21. For more information, see "Indonesia 2022," MWC, last modified January 1, 2021, https://mwc-cmm.org/assembly/indonesia-2022.

Interior of the Holy Stadium in Semarang, home of the JKI Gospel of the Kingdom church (JKI Injil Kerajaan) and site of the Mennonite World Conference global assembly in July 2022. PHOTOGRAPH COURTESY OF MENNONITE WORLD CONFERENCE

of the Anabaptist-Mennonite church, as several thousand brothers and sisters in Christ gather from more than fifty countries.

This book offers a brief introduction to the GITJ, GKMI, and JKI church conferences (or synods, as they are known in Indonesia) within the larger context of Indonesian history and culture. Although intended primarily as a resource for those who will be gathering in Semarang for the 17th MWC assembly, the story that follows may also be of interest to anyone who wants to know a little bit more about the character of Anabaptist-Mennonite movement as it has found expression in the Indonesian context. Additional resources, including a map of north Central Java just before this chapter and a sampling of recipes at the back of this book, may be useful for both attendees of the MWC assembly and armchair travelers.

If you have already visited Indonesia or have some understanding of the country's rich history, you will quickly recognize that this small book is quite limited in its scope. It focuses primarily on the island of Java—since that is where the overwhelming majority of Anabaptist-Mennonites live—paying little heed to the fascinating history and cultural attractions of the other six thousand inhabited islands in the vast archipelago that makes up the country.

Furthermore, members of the GITJ, GKMI, and JKI synods will almost certainly be disappointed at the brevity with which I treat the history of their individual groups. Significant names, places, and events that loom large in local memory are almost certainly missing from this account, either because of space limitations or my own ignorance. I have read as many English language sources as I could find on the history of the synods—drawing especially on the significant work of Lawrence Yoder, Sigit Heru Sukoco, Adhi Dharma, Adi Sutanto, Alle Hoekema, Andios Santoso, Paulus Widjaja, and other writers. I have consulted with Indonesian church leaders and historians for their perspectives, and I am deeply indebted to Sunoko Lin, who helped to facilitate visits to JKI congregations in the Los Angeles area, and to Daniel (Dante) Talenta, who accompanied me on a ten-day visit to Indonesia in the fall of 2019. But this is not an exhaustive account. The interpretation of events that I offer here is undoubtedly shaped by the limits of my own cultural perspectives and by the nature of the audience for whom the book is written. Readers should regard this text as an appetizer, not the main course. And should you encounter Indonesian church members who tell the story differently, always trust their version over mine!

The churches of Indonesia offer a fascinating window into the richness of the global Anabaptist-Mennonite church. I hope very much that you can participate in the MWC assembly in

Semarang in the summer of 2022. But if that is not possible, then I hope you will still commit yourself to reimagining the church in a global—rather than national—context, and that you will seek out, nourish, and celebrate every possible connection you can make with sisters and brothers who express their faith in ways that are different from your own.

Why attend the MWC Global Assembly in Semarang, Indonesia?

1. *Come to the MWC assembly to learn more about the global church.* We sometimes forget that the body of Christ is bigger than our congregation or national conference. The gathering in Semarang, Indonesia, in July 2022 offers a rare opportunity to learn more about the life and faith of sister churches in other countries. In addition to the wonderful international music and inspirational worship gatherings, you will have a chance to participate in a host of workshops, browse the booths at the Global Village pavilion, check in on the Global Youth Summit, and encounter church leaders from the 107 groups who are members of MWC. Doing so will give you a fuller picture of who we are as a global Anabaptist-Mennonite church. You will return home wanting to learn more.

2. *Come to the MWC assembly to renew friendships.* According to a recent survey of MC USA congregations, nearly 40 percent of our churches have a relationship with a sister church outside of the United States, and 76 percent include members who have served in international settings with MCC or a Mennonite-related mission agency.[22] The

---

22. John D. Roth, "MCUSA Survey Reveals Global Connections," *Rhizome: Updates from the Institute for the Study of Global Anabaptism* 1 (June 2014), 5.

same is true of most congregations in MC USA, MC Canada, the Church of the Brethren in the United States and Canada, and the Mennonite churches in Europe. Assembly 17 is a wonderful opportunity for you and your congregation to strengthen these longtime international friendships with face-to-face encounters.

3. *Come to the MWC assembly to make new friends.* Anyone who has traveled internationally knows the joy of unexpected, sometimes life-changing, relationships, seemingly formed by accident, that open up the world in a new way. Participants in Assembly 17 will have a chance to meet regularly for conversation in internationally diverse discussion groups. Meals, workshops, recreational activities, and Assembly Scattered tour options will provide dozens of additional opportunities to meet other participants. Go to Assembly 17 assuming that you will exchange phone numbers, email addresses, and social media links. The connections you make could blossom into lifelong cross-cultural friendships.

4. *Come to the MWC assembly to be renewed and transformed.* Our congregations and conferences in Europe and North America have been facing difficult times in recent years. Sometimes it's difficult to be hopeful about the future. At Assembly 17 you will encounter Mennonite brothers and sisters from churches around the world who are also facing enormous challenges—poverty, limited access to education, COVID-19 and other health crises, profound political instability, and even persecution. The looming crisis of climate change affects all of us, albeit in very uneven ways. Come to Assembly 17 with the goal of listening and sharing, ready to bear one another's burdens, and to be renewed by Christ's promise that he will never leave or forsake his people.

5. *Come to the MWC assembly to receive hospitality.* The story of the early church is filled with accounts of Christians extending hospitality to each other as they traveled across cultures and languages. Hospitality is a fundamental Christian virtue. If you have spent time abroad—as a tourist, as a short-term volunteer, or on a study tour—you almost certainly remember times when you experienced a gracious and generous reception from others. Members of the GITJ, GKMI, and JKI synods in Indonesia have expressed their eagerness to extend Christian hospitality to brothers and sisters from around the world. And regardless of whether you are able to attend in person, you could extend your own hospitality with a financial gift that will make it possible for others to attend the gathering.

6. *Finally, come to the MWC assembly to discover the cultural richness of Indonesia.* The Republic of Indonesia is the world's fourth most populous country, famous for its wood carving, batik, shadow puppets, and traditional dance, and home to some of the most stunning natural beauty to be found anywhere in the world. The world's largest population of Muslims resides in Indonesia; but the country's strong national commitment to religious freedom has also enabled smaller Buddhist, Hindu, Confucian, and Christian communities to flourish as well. For many people, Indonesia is an affordable destination, with an excellent infrastructure for tourists, who will enjoy the flavorful cuisine, remarkable cultural diversity, and friendly reception.

2

An Introduction to Indonesia

*B*Y THE RULES of ordinary logic, the country of Indonesia should not exist.

Stretching along the earth's equator for 3,200 miles—the distance from New York City to Lima, Peru—Indonesia comprises a chain of roughly seventeen thousand islands that extend from the western tip of Sumatra in the Indian Ocean eastward to the island of New Guinea in the Pacific Ocean.[23] Although nearly 60 percent of Indonesia's 270 million inhabitants make their home on the central island of Java, Indonesians living on islands like Sumatra, Kalimantan, Sulawesi, Maluku, Papua, Nusa Tenggara, and Bali also claim a rich and distinctive identity. Across the archipelago, people speak between six hundred and seven hundred different languages and identify with at least 360 ethnic groups.

---

23. A minor controversy exists around determining the exact number of islands in Indonesia, since many of the smaller land masses appear and disappear with the tide. Some sources cite only thirteen thousand islands. Around six thousand of the islands are inhabited.

For centuries, the region was the focus of powerful outside civilizations—Melanesian, Chinese, Indian, Arab, European—each leaving a distinctive cultural and religious imprint on some part of the vast archipelago, with some of the visitors seeking to actively divide and colonize its people. And even though the overwhelming majority of Indonesia's inhabitants today are Muslim, the forms of Islam they embrace vary widely, and strong elements of Hinduism, Buddhism, Confucianism, and Christianity remain deeply embedded in the culture.

Yet somehow, despite all this geographical, cultural, and religious diversity, the scattered inhabitants of the world's fourth most populous nation have developed a shared national identity. Indonesians today are joined by a common national language (Bahasa Indonesian), a growing modern economy, slowly maturing democratic institutions, and a shared commitment to the national motto of "unity in diversity" (Bhinneka Tunggal Ika). Although the recent history of Indonesia has also included periods of intense ethnic violence, religious extremism, and a military dictatorship, the larger picture of Indonesia today is one of a peaceful culture with a remarkable capacity to accommodate and integrate differences, while also preserving strong regional and local identities.

The history of Indonesia unfolds like an archaeological dig in which each layer reveals an essential, interrelated part of the whole.[24] Over the centuries, waves of outside empires and religions have left their distinctive marks on Indonesian culture,

---

24. The basic information that follows in this history draws from a variety of sources, including Tim Hannigan, *A Brief History of Indonesia: Sultan, Spices and Tsunamis* (Rutland, VT: Tuttle Publishing, 2015); Robert Cribb and Colin Brown, *Modern Indonesia: A History since 1945* (New York: Longman Publishing, 1995); and Colin Brown, *A Short History of Indonesia: The Unlikely Nation?* (Crows Nest, AU: Allen and Unwin, 2003).

even as they were, in turn, absorbed and reshaped by subsequent political and religious forces. As a nation of many islands, the separation imposed by sea encouraged a proliferation of distinctive local traditions. But the same waters that divide groups from each other also serve as a bridge ensuring that the cultures of seafaring people in search of trade will inevitably interact with each other. Although a unified national identity did not emerge until the twentieth century, Indonesia has always been united by the many civilizations and religions that have interacted with its people for at least three millennia.

For modern visitors, the history of Indonesia is best summarized in three major periods: the earliest recorded indigenous settlements, with strong influences from Melanesia, India, and China; the era of European colonization (1500–1945); and Indonesia's independence and the emergence of a modern nation (1945–present).

EARLY SETTLEMENTS

The chain of islands forming modern Indonesia emerged from the sea some 250 million years ago as a result of volcanic activity along the Indo-Australian tectonic plate that forms part of the so-called Ring of Fire. The island of Java—located close to the geographic center of the archipelago, and claiming some of the most fertile soil in all of southeast Asia—was formed almost entirely by volcanoes; indeed, 45 of its 65 volcanoes are still active today. Once exposed to air, the rich volcanic soil quickly nourished the growth of dense jungles, teeming with an astounding variety of plant and animal life.

Recent paleontological discoveries suggest that among the earliest inhabitants of Indonesia were a highly distinct group of hominids, dubbed *Homo floresiensis*, for the island of Flores where their skeletal remains and the stone shards they created approximately one hundred thousand years ago were first discovered. Standing only around three feet tall, *Homo floresiensis* has been dubbed the Flores Hobbit, and continues to be a source of great interest and debate among paleo-anthropologists.[25]

The first modern humans to settle the islands were likely Austronesians from what is now Australia or New Zealand who arrived in the eastern part of archipelago some twelve thousand years ago. They were followed approximately six to seven thousand years later by Melanesians from the Philippines or Taiwan who introduced dogs, pigs, pottery, buffalo, and, crucially, rice culture. These peoples settled first on the large island of Sulawesi, but then gradually formed villages and scattered settlements in Java, Sumatra, Timor, and Borneo. At some later point, other immigrants introduced metalworking skills that suggest they arrived from what is now Vietnam.

By the time of Christ, an international trade network was emerging—driven by seasonal changes in the sea currents linking the Indian Ocean with the South China Sea—that slowly transformed the Indonesian archipelago into an important setting for encounters between Indian and Chinese empires. During the Han Dynasty in China (ca. 200 BCE–200 CE), for example, small communities of Indian and Chinese traders emerged in ports throughout the archipelago. Chinese culture, and waves of immigrants from China, have left a deep imprint on Indonesia ever since.

---

25. See, for example, G. van den Bergh, Y. Kaifu, I. Kurniawan, et al., "*Homo floresiensis*-like Fossils from the Early Middle Pleistocene of Flores," *Nature* 534 (2016): 245–48. The fossil remains of the so-called "Java Man" (*Homo erectus erectus*), discovered in the 1890s, suggest the presence of an even earlier hominid group.

Sometime around 600 CE, influences from India became stronger—particularly in Sumatra, Java, and Bali—with the slow introduction of Sanskrit, the construction of Hindu temples, and distinctive irrigation systems for the cultivation of rice. If the Chinese left behind traces of Confucianism, the religious legacy of India can be seen in the prevalence of Buddhism and Hinduism in some parts of the country still today. The ninth-century Sailendra dynasty in Java, for example, created the remarkable structure of Borobudur, the largest Buddhist temple in the world. Located close to Muntilan in Central Java, the Borobudur temple integrates classic Gupta Indian architecture with indigenous Indonesian design elements. Equally impressive is the Hindu temple complex of Prambanan, located northeast of the city of Yogyakarta, that preserves vestiges of the Mataram dynasty from later in the ninth century. In the late thirteenth century, the Hindu Majapahit kingdom, with its center in eastern Java, pursued a policy of political and economic conquest that eventually included some ninety-eight tributary states, including much of southeast Asia. Historians sometimes refer to this period, from 1293 to circa 1527, as a "Golden Age" in Indonesian history.

The origins of Islam in Indonesia are a source of much debate among scholars.[26] Were its roots in India or the Arabian Peninsula? Did it arrive in the ninth century or the thirteenth century? How quickly was it adopted by villagers? And in what form? What is known is that by the end of the thirteenth century, Islam was well established in North Sumatra, and was similarly rooted in Java by the following century. Other parts

26. Cf. M. C. Ricklefs, *Islamisation and Its Opponents in Java* (Singapore: University of Hawaii Press, 2012).

of the archipelago also gradually adopted Islam—first in port cities and then elsewhere as merchants traveled to the interior and religious leaders began to establish boarding schools (*pesantren*) to teach the Qur'an. A clear turning point occurred in the early sixteenth century when the Hindu Majapahit empire in Java fell to the Demak Sultanate, a Muslim state centered on Java's north coast. After the fall of the Majapahit empire, many Hindus who fled Java found refuge in Bali, which remains the primary center of Hindu culture and religion still today. In 1527, the Muslim sultan renamed the newly conquered city of Sunda Kelapa as Jayakarta (meaning "precious victory"), which was eventually contracted to Jakarta, Java's largest city and the capital of Indonesia.

By the reign of Sultan Agung of Mataram (1613–1645), virtually all the older Hindu-Buddhist kingdoms of Indonesia had converted, at least nominally, to Islam. In Java and Sumatra, Islam was clearly the dominant religion, present in villages, favored by merchants and traders, and well established among government officials. At the same time, Muslim beliefs and practices were always overlaid and mixed with persistent currents of Hindu-Buddhism and indigenous forms of animism that revered ancestral spirits and regarded features of the natural landscape—trees, stones, mountains, bodies of water—as sacred sites, imbued with spirits.

Today, Indonesia is the world's most populous Muslim-majority country, with nearly 90 percent of its population—or 227 million people—identifying as Muslim. The overwhelming majority are Sunni, although many adherents, particularly in Java, identify with a form of Islam heavily influenced by Sufism (Kebatinan) that emphasizes inner reflection and a spiritual closeness with God.

In general, all religions in Indonesia have been influenced by a traditional, somewhat fatalistic view of life, in which larger forces are at work to shape nature and society and the individual's destiny is determined by fate. This orientation means that Indonesians have traditionally focused less on individual agency and choices and more on the larger challenge of maintaining social balance and harmony. Thus, the Javanese *slametan*—a ceremonial meal celebrated with neighbors or community members—is filled with rituals that promote social unity and mutual aid, beginning with the extended family, and moving then to the village and the larger community. In one way or another, these themes find expression in all the religions practiced in Indonesia today.

EUROPEAN COLONIZATION

The dominant Muslim character of Indonesia continued long after the arrival of the Europeans in 1512 and the introduction of Christianity. The first Europeans to make contact with the islands were Portuguese traders in search of spices. In the early decades of the sixteenth century, as Europeans enthusiastically embraced the new tastes of nutmeg, cloves, and pepper in their diet, the Portuguese extended their presence in the archipelago. Through a combination of military conquest and alliances with local rulers, they established trading posts, forts, and Catholic missions, especially in the Maluku (or Spice) Islands of Ternate and Ambon. Dutch and British merchants soon followed, seeking their own claims to the lucrative spice markets in the "East Indies."

By the end of the sixteenth century, the Dutch were emerging as the dominant European presence in the region. When a Dutch expedition to the East Indies in 1597 made a

400 percent profit on spice trade, the Dutch government, recognizing the commercial potential of the region, merged all the companies into the United East India Company (Vereenigde Oost-Indische Compagnie, or VOC), a share-holding enterprise focused almost exclusively on exporting spices and other goods from Indonesia.[27] Over the next 350 years—from the late sixteenth century to the declaration of independence in 1945—the Dutch exerted a powerful influence over the early modern history of Indonesia.[28]

The process of Dutch colonization was slow and uneven. Dutch control was strongest in Java, as representatives of the VOC pitted local leaders against each other with trade deals, bribes, and threats amid the collapse of the Mataram empire.[29] The city of Jakarta—renamed Batavia by the Dutch—became a vibrant hub of economic and political power, with a steady stream of spices, wood, and other commodities flowing from Java and neighboring islands to Dutch ports. In 1796, a combination of mismanagement, corruption, and fierce competition from the English East India Company led to the shocking bankruptcy of the VOC. As a result the Dutch crown nationalized the company's holdings and assumed outright sovereignty over the island of Java. For a short time, in the aftermath of the French Revolution, the British claimed control of the

---

27. One of the first reports of the Western encounter with the islands of Indonesia was written by Aernoudt Lintgens, a young Mennonite merchant and sailor who accompanied Cornelis de Houtman's 1597 expedition and described his impressions of the island of Bali. Cf. Margaret J. Wiener, *Visible and Invisible Realms: Power, Magic and Colonial Conquest in Bali* (Chicago: University of Chicago Press, 1995).

28. Kwee Hui Kian, "How Strangers Became Kings," *Indonesia and the Malay World* 36 (2008): 293–307.

29. Many areas remained independent throughout much of this time, including Aceh, Bali, Lombok, and Borneo.

archipelago, but after Napoleon's defeat at Waterloo in 1815, the Dutch were able to reassert their colonial claims.

In the course of the nineteenth century, the Dutch government extended its political and economic control beyond Java to include the outer islands, clearly transforming the Dutch East Indies into a nationalized colony. In Java, Dutch administrators introduced a system of forced labor, as a means of extracting taxes from Javanese villagers by forcing them to work on Dutch-owned plantations. Under this system, 20 percent of village land had to be devoted to government crops for export. Javanese peasants, who were forced to work on the plantations for sixty days of the year, faced new travel restrictions. The Dutch also claimed a monopoly on the lucrative coffee market, forbidding the Javanese to plant coffee. And they imposed the Dutch legal system, negotiated trade deals that divided royal families against each other, and employed immigrants from China as tax collectors and administrators, thereby fostering ethnic tensions that would continue to fester well into the twentieth century.[30]

Nevertheless, Dutch political control over the archipelago was always tenuous. Their policies, especially those related to forced labor, sparked numerous local rebellions as well as nationalist movements attempting to unite all Indonesians against Dutch rule. In 1825, for example, a Javanese prince named Diponegoro led an armed rebellion that drew widespread support from both the rural population and the aristocracy. Although Diponegoro surrendered in 1830, the guerrilla campaign cost the lives of some two hundred thousand Javanese and fifteen thousand soldiers in the Dutch colonial army. In

---

30. To be sure, many of these ethnic Chinese "immigrants" had lived in Java for generations, and large numbers worked as laborers on VOC plantations.

the decades that followed, the uprising would inspire later generations of Javanese nationalists to undertake similar forms of resistance to the Dutch colonial government.[31]

As we will explore in subsequent chapters, it is impossible to understand the nature of Mennonite missions and the complex history of the Anabaptist-Mennonite churches that emerged apart from this context of colonial exploitation, dependency, competing ethnic identities, and rising nationalism.

INDONESIAN INDEPENDENCE AND THE EMERGENCE OF MODERN INDONESIA

In 1901, Queen Wilhelmina introduced a new strategy—the so-called Ethical Policy—as part of a larger effort to address social and economic inequities in all Dutch colonies, including the East Indies. Prior to 1901, the Dutch colonial government had actively discouraged Indonesians from learning Dutch, preferring to conduct business in Javanese or Malay, a trade language widely used throughout the archipelago. Indeed, in the 1890s only a tiny fraction—perhaps 150 thousand out of a total population of 40 million—were enrolled in government primary schools. With the introduction of the Ethical Policy, however, this slowly began to change. Though chronically underfunded, a growing number of schools began to identify gifted Javanese students for training in Dutch as future civil servants.

It was from the ranks of this new generation of Dutch-speaking, educated Javanese that the first organized political movements began to emerge, raising critical questions about

---

31. Peter Carey, "Waiting for the 'Just King': The Agrarian World of South-Central Java from Giyanti (1755) to the Java War (1825–30)," *Modern Asian Studies* 20, no. 1 (Feb. 1986): 59–137.

the future of Indonesia and introducing the language of rights, freedom, and liberty into public conversations. One early expression of this new political consciousness was the formation in 1908 of Beautiful Endeavor (Budi Utomo), a student-run organization that pressed for greater access to university education.

Three years later, the Islamic Trade Union (Sarekat Dagang Islam) emerged in Surakarta, as an effort by Javanese traders and merchants to resist domination of local markets by their Chinese neighbors. In 1912, the Indies Party (Indische Partij) coalesced with the explicit goal of outright independence from Dutch rule. For the first time, Javanese intellectuals began to embrace the concept of "Indonesia," not just as a geographical description, but as a vision for a unified nation-state free from outside control. These various organizations gradually became popular movements, thanks in part to rising rates of literacy and the growing number of Malay-language newspapers that began to appear in the early 1920s.

This was the context in which Sukarno[32]—generally regarded as the father of modern Indonesia—burst into the national consciousness as a kind of force of nature. Sukarno was both a Muslim and a student of Marxist theory. In addition to being a remarkably gifted orator, Sukarno astutely devised a vision for a pragmatic nationalism, anchored in a loosely secular socialism, that could speak to the economic oppression of Indonesian peasants while also forging alliances across the religious and cultural diversity of the archipelago.

---

32. Indonesian naming conventions are often confusing to Western people. Some use only one name; sometimes names are prefaced by the honorific Pak or Bu, and sometimes people change their names. I do not use honorifics, but since it sounds odd to treat the second name of an Indonesian as a family name, I generally include the full name in each reference to an individual Indonesian.

In 1926, Sukarno and other young, educated Indonesians formed a political party—the Indonesian Nationalist Association (Perserikatan Nasional Indonesia, or PNI)—and a second umbrella organization called the Union of Political Organizations of the Indonesian People (PPPKI) to provide an organizational structure for implementing their demands. At a famous gathering in October 1928, leaders of the emerging movement committed themselves to the Youth Pledge (Sumpah Pemuda), which expressed their hopes with a disarming simplicity: "We, the sons and daughters of Indonesia, acknowledge one motherland, Indonesia . . . one nation, the nation of Indonesia . . . and uphold the language of unity, Indonesian." Together with Mohammad Hatta, who emerged as the young nationalists' leading intellectual, Sukarno channeled the frustrations and yearnings of his generation into a political movement. Not surprisingly, Dutch authorities reacted allergically to the growing nationalist movement, imprisoning Sukarno, Hatta, and other leaders in isolated settings far from Batavia/Jakarta.

At that point, global events took center stage. In 1930, the economic tsunami of the Great Depression crashed over Indonesia, forcing people to attend to matters of basic survival. Meanwhile, in 1931, Japan invaded Manchuria, and in distant Europe, Hitler was rising to power in Germany. On May 10, 1940, Hitler invaded the Netherlands, cutting off the East Indies from its political and economic ties to Holland. Seven months later, Japan—by then an ally with Germany—launched an attack on Hong Kong and Malaysia. By the early spring of 1942, Dutch forces in Java surrendered to the Japanese, bringing an end to nearly 350 years of Dutch rule.

Overnight, the Japanese occupiers forbade any use— public or private—of the Dutch language. Streets, hotels, and restaurants were renamed; the city of Batavia reverted to the name Jakarta; and Bahasa Indonesian became the country's official language. Most of the Dutch citizens living in the archipelago were interned in prison camps for the duration of the war. In the vacuum of power that initially ensued, violence erupted in the Javanese countryside, especially against Christians and the local Chinese community, groups that many Javanese regarded as collaborators with the Dutch colonialists.

Although greeted as liberators, in many ways the Japanese were at least as oppressive and brutal as the Dutch. Perhaps as many as two million Indonesians died of hunger during the three and a half years of Japanese occupation. Nevertheless, the heroes of the nationalist movement—people like Sukarno and Hatta—found it more palatable to collaborate with the Japanese than to support a return to Dutch rule. In the spring of 1945, when the tides of World War II shifted decisively against Germany and Japan, Sukarno and others formed the Committee for Preparatory Work for Indonesian Independence. In a famous speech on June 1, 1945, Sukarno outlined what he called the Pancasila (the Five Principles) as the official unifying foundation of the new nation that he envisioned. The Pancasila—which continues to be recited today by schoolchildren and emblazoned on seals, coins, and public buildings—includes the following principles:

1. belief in the One True God, with freedom of worship[33]

2. a fair-minded and civilized humanity

---

33. While the constitution stipulates religious freedom, the government officially recognizes only six religions: Islam, Protestantism, Roman Catholicism, Hinduism, Buddhism, and Confucianism, with indigenous religions acknowledged only informally.

3. the unity of Indonesia

4. representative democracy

5. social justice

Almost immediately after Japan surrendered to the Allies in August 1945—after the United States dropped atomic bombs on Hiroshima and Nagasaki—Indonesia declared its independence as the united Republic of Indonesia. President Sukarno and vice president Mohammad Hatta promised to build a nation on the foundation of the Pancasila.[34]

For the next four years, Indonesians fought a bitter struggle—both armed and diplomatic—first against the British, who temporarily stepped in as the administrators of postwar Indonesia, and then against the Dutch, who sought to reimpose their colonial rule. Finally, on December 27, 1949, under pressure from the United Nations and the judgment of the world community, the Dutch formally recognized Indonesia as an independent state.[35]

As president, Sukarno's genius was to consolidate power by managing a delicate balance between Indonesian nationalism, political Islam, and the most radical political party, the Communist Party of Indonesia (Partai Komunis Indonesia, or PKI). In the end, the transition to democracy proved to be very messy, and often at odds with the vision that Sukarno had promised citizens of the new country. Some eighty political

---

34. Initially, Indonesia functioned as a federation of provinces. The actual Republic of Indonesia did not come into existence in a formal way until August 17, 1950—exactly five years after the declaration of independence in 1945.

35. The Dutch retained control over the western half of the island of New Guinea. In 1963, the Netherlands turned over political control of the region to Indonesia, setting off a long and bloody civil war.

parties vied for power, each competing for the support of a population with only a 10 percent literacy rate in 1950.[36]

By the mid-1950s, Sukarno declared parliamentary democracy to be a Western affectation. Instead, he argued for a model of "Guided Democracy," rooted in traditional Indonesian practices of "discussion and consensus," in which he would serve as the paternalistic national village chief. In March 1957, when regional military commanders rebelled in Sumatra, Sukarno used the incident as an excuse to declare martial law. At the same time, he ordered the expulsion of nearly fifty thousand Dutch citizens, renounced the national debt to the Netherlands, and nationalized Dutch assets. Even more ominously, Sukarno repatriated thousands of ethnic Chinese businesspeople—many of whom had lived in Indonesia for generations—to China. In 1963, he declared himself "Leader for Life" and resorted to increasingly bellicose speeches—denouncing American cultural influence, for example, or threatening to invade Malaysia—in order to whip up demonstrations among his supporters in Jakarta. As Sukarno's policies became more authoritarian, popular support for the Communist party, the PKI, rapidly grew on the Left, whereas traditional landowners and business leaders found allies on the Right, either among military leaders in the Indonesian National Army or within an awakening Islamic political movement.

These tensions culminated in a paroxysm of violence in the fall of 1965 that marked a further shift toward authoritarian rule. Most historians now agree that the coup attempt initiated on September 30—allegedly planned by the PKI against Sukarno—was actually instigated by junior officers in Sukarno's

---

36. According to official statistics, the literacy rate in Indonesia was only 5 percent in 1945, but had risen to 47 percent by 1961.

own army.[37] Blaming the events on the PKI provided an excuse for government soldiers and local nationalist militia groups, led by General Suharto, to pursue a violent anticommunist purge that resulted in the massacre of somewhere between five hundred thousand and one million people, again many of them ethnic Chinese. When the pogrom ended, the military and Islamic groups had emerged as the clear winners. Indeed, General Suharto capitalized on the military's new role as a power broker and, after a drawn-out power play with Sukarno, was appointed president in March 1967.

Suharto's "New Order" administration, supported by the United States, encouraged foreign direct investment, which was a crucial factor in the subsequent three decades of substantial economic growth. At the same time, the fledgling democratic movement in Indonesia was forced underground. Emblematic of the authoritarian character of Suharto's rule was the decision in 1975 to invade East Timor and to declare it the twenty-seventh province of Indonesia. Officially, the action was intended to squelch remnants of communism in the region; but the twenty-five-year occupation that followed would become a financial burden and human rights disaster, marked by widespread international condemnation of human rights abuses there.[38] Other insurgencies in the provinces of Papua and Papua Barat (sometimes known as West New Guinea)—and, at the opposite end of the archipelago, among radicalized Muslims in Aceh—were also ruthlessly repressed.

---

37. Cf. John Roosa, *Pretext for Mass Murder: The September 30th Movement and Suharto's Coup d'État in Indonesia* (Madison, WI: University of Wisconsin Press, 2006).

38. In 1999, East Timor seceded from Indonesia.

Suharto also introduced new policies intended to force the assimilation of Chinese Indonesians. Ethnic Chinese, who comprised roughly 5 percent of the population, had long been the focus of intense resentment and hostility. Suharto's "New Order" attempted to assimilate Chinese Indonesians by banning the use of Chinese characters in public signage, closing Chinese newspapers and schools, outlawing traditional festivities, and forcing ethnic Chinese to adopt familiar Indonesian names.

At the same time, Indonesia underwent a period of remarkable economic growth under Suharto—some of it driven by massive logging operations in Kalimantan, oil extraction in Sumatra, copper and gold mining in Papua and Papua Barat, and the promise of cheap labor (e.g., factories producing T-shirts and running shoes). Indonesia was also ground zero for the so-called Green Revolution of the 1970s, which saw the introduction of new strains of seeds, pesticides, chemical fertilizers, and small armies of agricultural experts focused on the gospel of "development." As part of his plan to modernize Indonesia, Suharto rejoined the United Nations, restored relations with the United States, and entered into a host of trade agreements with Asian and European countries, all of which brought a new sense of economic stability and normalcy to the country. Under his rule, Indonesians could choose between three major political parties—the Muslim United Development Party (PPP), the Indonesian Democratic Party (PDI), and Suharto's own Golkar (Golongan Karya) party, to which all government employees and military personnel had to belong. Not surprisingly, every five years the Golkar party won elections by a landslide.

Economic growth under Suharto continued through the 1980s, marked by road construction, new schools, and the emergence of high-rise buildings in all of Java's major cities.

But corruption, which had always been part of Indonesian politics, became especially brazen among Suharto's extended family, prompting growing public criticism. And rumblings of a new militant strain of Islamic radicalism also began to challenge the syncretistic forms of Islam that had been part of Javanese religious life for centuries.

In 1997 Indonesia was devastated by the Asian financial crisis. The plunging value of the rupiah brought a halt to building projects, and the massive IMF loans used to bail out the Indonesian economy were conditioned on economic and political reforms. The crisis emboldened growing public criticism of government corruption, leading to student protests and then to efforts by the government to suppress all political opposition. As violence spilled into the streets, government security forces stood by as angry mobs once again expressed their frustrations in violence against the Chinese, openly looting Chinese-owned businesses, burning homes, and raping Chinese women and girls in Jakarta, Surakarta, Palembang, and elsewhere. On May 21, 1998, in the midst of the upheaval, Suharto resigned from the presidency and was replaced by his deputy B. J. Habibie.

In the post-Suharto era, democratic processes have been strengthened. Habibie freed political prisoners, permitted new political parties to form, removed restrictions on the press, separated the police from the army, and reduced the power of the military. He also granted East Timor the freedom to secede (albeit not without a final burst of chaotic violence by the military), and held free regional and parliament elections in July 1999. In 2004, the country celebrated its first direct presidential election.

Although political corruption, economic and social instability, and outbreaks of terrorism remained problems in the opening decades of the twenty-first century,[39] the Indonesian government has generally not exploited sectarian discontent and violence for political gain. In 2005, for example, the government successfully negotiated a political settlement to an armed separatist conflict in the island of Aceh, after a devastating earthquake and tsunami killed over 130 thousand people in the region.

In 2014, Joko Widodo (known as Jokowi), a popular mayor of the Javanese city of Surabaya, was elected as Indonesia's president on an anticorruption and reformist platform. Reelected to a second five-year term in 2019, Jokowi faces significant challenges. Serious concerns about rising sea levels, for example, have prompted the government to embark on a massive plan to move the country's capital from Jakarta to a newly created city on the island of Kalimantan, a move that may also ease the deep resentment in the provinces against the political and economic dominance of Java. Ongoing corruption, a strained infrastructure, concerns about radicalized Islam, and the challenges of environmental degradation—including large-scale illegal logging in Kalimantan and massive deforestation in Sumatra—are real. But even in the face of these challenges, today the world's fourth most populous country can claim a modern, dynamic economy, mostly democratic institutions, and a rich cultural vitality.[40]

The history and identity of the Anabaptist-Mennonite communities in Indonesia cannot be understood apart from these larger currents. A long tradition of religious diversity, the

39. In 1999–2000, for example, a severe outburst of religious violence between Christians and radical Muslim groups took place at Ambon and elsewhere in the Moluccan islands.

40. Only China, India, and the United States have populations larger than Indonesia.

painful legacy of Dutch colonial rule, the rise of Indonesian nationalism, and a history of ethnic tension that has frequently spilled over into violence against the Chinese community all helped to shape the contours of the GITJ, GKMI, and JKI churches. In the same way, the opportunities and challenges that these churches face today are unfolding in the context of a rapidly modernizing, predominantly Muslim country, as Indonesia finds its way within a larger geopolitical world dominated by India, China, and the United States.

3

Before Pieter Jansz There Was Tunggul Wulung:

The Early History of the Javanese Mennonite Church

*I*N THE STANDARD telling of the story, the history of Anabaptist-Mennonite churches in Indonesia nearly always begins with an account of the Dutch Mennonite Mission Board and the work of their first missionary, Pieter Jansz, who, along with his wife, Wilhelmina, arrived in Indonesia in November 1851.[41] In that version of the story, the baptisms of five Javanese believers in Jepara, on the northern coast of Central Java, on April 16, 1854, marked the beginnings of the first Mennonite church whose members were not primarily of European background.

---

41. See, for example, C. J. Dyck, *An Introduction to Mennonite History* (Scottdale, PA: Herald Press, 1967), 258–59; or Horst Penner, *Weltweite Bruderschaft: Ein mennonitisches Geschichtsbuch*, 3rd ed. (Karlsruhe, Germany: Verlag Heinrich Schneider, 1972).

In the years that followed, Jansz worked tirelessly as a preacher, teacher, administrator, and scholar. In 1888 he completed the first translation of the New Testament into Javanese, and he was instrumental in creating a Dutch-Javanese dictionary. Thus Jansz, who was succeeded in the Mennonite Mission in 1881 by his son Pieter Anthonie Jansz, is frequently identified as the father of the Mennonite-related churches in Indonesia. From these roots sprang three synods—GITJ, GKMI, and JKI—whose membership in Mennonite World Conference and whose close connections with European and North American mission and relief agencies have anchored their identity as significant members in the global Anabaptist-Mennonite fellowship.

That story is not entirely wrong. As we shall see, Pieter Jansz and the missionaries who served under the Dutch Mennonite Mission did indeed have a significant impact on the character of the three Indonesian synods that are members of Mennonite World Conference today. But this version of the story is also somewhat misleading.

In the first place, the narrative tends to overlook the complex history of Christianity in Indonesia that preceded Jansz's arrival and helped shape the identity of the churches that emerged. Since the early sixteenth century, various European countries struggled for supremacy over the spice-rich islands. In 1522, the Portuguese missionary Francis Xavier claimed the region for Catholicism and oversaw the construction of churches defended by a series of Portuguese forts on the eastern edge of the archipelago. In 1605, when the Dutch succeeded the Portuguese as the dominant European power, the United East India Trading Company (VOC) paid pastors to establish Reformed churches in the Javanese port cities of Batavia, Semarang, and Surabaya.

Over the next three centuries, Dutch colonial administrators in Indonesia promoted the theology, liturgy, and architecture of the Dutch Reformed Church, represented by the Dutch Missionary Society (Nederlandsch Zendeling Genootschap), as well as the more conservative Gereformeerde Church. Following the French Revolution, when control over the islands shifted momentarily into the hands of the French, Catholicism regained a foothold. Then British administrators, who ruled from 1811 to 1816, encouraged missionaries of the Baptist Missionary Society to establish outposts in Java and elsewhere throughout the archipelago. So when Pieter Jansz arrived in the village of Jepara in north Central Java in the early 1850s, Christianity was already well established in the region, albeit as a minority religion.[42]

These circumstances had several consequences for the future trajectory of the Anabaptist-Mennonite churches that emerged in Indonesia. In the first place, Christianity in mid-nineteenth-century Indonesia was inseparable from the long history of European colonization. This meant that when Jansz arrived in Java, the gospel he intended to share could not be easily distinguished from the visible signs of Dutch power—including forced labor obligations and all the other humiliations and inequities associated with Dutch colonial occupation. To his credit, Jansz immediately threw himself into the task of learning Javanese; he was attentive to Javanese culture; he was generally critical of the forced labor system that kept so many

---

42. Although Christianity remained a very small minority in Java, elsewhere in Indonesia—especially on the islands of Papua, the Moluccas, Timor, Flores, and North Sumatra—it had a much stronger presence. Cf. Jan Sihar Aritonang and Karel Steenbrink, eds., *A History of Christianity in Indonesia* (Leiden: Brill, 2008).

Javanese villagers in poverty; and he insisted that his primary vocation was that of a schoolteacher, not an evangelist.

But in the eyes of most local Javanese, Jansz and the Mennonite Mission, funded by supporters in the Netherlands, were simply an extension of the Dutch colonial government. Indeed, early Javanese participants in the Mennonite mission churches routinely distinguished between "Dutch Christians" (Kristen Londo) and "Javanese Christians" (Kristen Jawa). To be sure, Dutch and German Mennonite missionaries refused to accept this distinction, regarding the church as one body. But there was no way to deny the significant differences in power, resources, and authority that set the missionaries apart from Javanese members in the first seventy-five years of the church's existence.

Second, because the overwhelming majority of Indonesians practiced some form of Islam, Christians in the region, as a numerical minority, tended to regard each other first and foremost as fellow believers, and only secondarily as members of a distinctive denomination. Although the various Christian Unions that formed in the early twentieth century tended to be dominated by the Reformed Church, Indonesian churches in Java did not generally adopt strong denominational identities as Baptists, Lutherans, Methodists, or Mennonites. For Jansz and his missionary colleagues, the Anabaptist-Mennonite practice of adult, rather than infant, baptism was the most visible point of difference, and the churches they nurtured tended to place a strong emphasis on instruction before admitting new members. But for the most part, markers of denominational identity in Java were less pronounced than they were in Europe or North America.

The most important reason to qualify the traditional focus on the pioneering efforts of Pieter and Wilhelmina Jansz, however, is the central role that several key Javanese leaders played in establishing the churches that ultimately flourished in Java.[43] As Jansz soon discovered, church growth in the Muria region of Java was almost entirely dependent on the efforts of local lay evangelists. The Dutch missionaries could import European Mennonite theological convictions, confessions of faith, catechisms, church polities, and architectural styles; and they could establish and staff schools, clinics, and hospitals. But the early Indonesian converts who were baptized into the congregations that Jansz and his fellow missionaries were attempting to establish remained firmly anchored in Javanese culture, including traditional forms of religion. The churches that emerged were largely the result of the evangelistic efforts of Javanese preachers; and those congregations continued to be deeply shaped by Javanese cultural realities.

The Javanese leaders who were largely responsible for the converts in the first decades of the church's existence have remained virtually hidden from view in part because they left far fewer written sources than the Dutch missionaries, but also because they were never ordained or formally recognized as leaders. Indeed, the Dutch Mission would not ordain the first Javanese pastor until 1929, more than 75 years after Jansz arrived. Although it might have appeared from the outside that the growth of the church was due mostly to the efforts of Dutch and German missionaries, nothing could be further from the truth.

---

43. This is a primary theme in Sigit Heru Sukoco and Lawrence M. Yoder, *The Way of the Gospel in the World of Java: A History of the Muria Javanese Mennonite Church (GITJ)* (Goshen, IN: Institute for the Study of Global Anabaptism, 2020). Alle Hoekema has also underscored the significance of Javanese Christians in the early history of the Mennonite mission. See, for example, Alle Hoekema, "Developments in the Education of Preachers in the Indonesian Mennonite Churches," *Mennonite Quarterly Review* 59 (Oct. 1985): 398–400.

Clearly, Pieter Jansz, his son Anthonie Pieter Jansz, and the score of Dutch and German missionaries who labored in Java through the middle of the twentieth century played a crucial role in the history of the Anabaptist-Mennonite churches of Indonesia. Their contributions, often made at some personal cost, were significant. But the missionaries were catalysts and collaborators. And their legacy—for all their sacrifice and good intentions—was complex and often ambiguous.

THE MISSIONARY CHARACTER OF THE ANABAPTIST MOVEMENT

The foray of the Dutch Mennonite Mission Society into the larger Protestant mission movement in the middle of the nineteenth century was rooted in a much deeper Anabaptist missionary tradition going back to the sixteenth century. In contrast to the dominant Christian traditions of the time, Anabaptist leaders in the sixteenth century were convinced that no one—not even in "Christian Europe"—was born a Christian. Babies could be baptized, of course, but that ritual did not instantly transform them into followers of Jesus. Instead, Anabaptists believed, every individual needed to count the cost of what it would mean to follow in the way of Jesus and to make a conscious choice to accept the gift of love, forgiveness, and grace that God freely offered. For them, the ritual of baptism that followed conversion also marked a commitment to join with fellow Christians in reading Scripture together and actively discerning how it should be applied to their daily life.

This understanding of baptism was deeply threatening to the Catholic, Lutheran, and Reformed neighbors of the Anabaptists in the sixteenth century who continued to practice infant baptism. Equally unsettling were Anabaptist teachings, drawn especially from the Sermon on the Mount, that called Christians to share possessions, reject oaths, and love their enemies. Together, these convictions seemed to undermine the very foundations of the Christian tradition and the stability of social, economic, and political order. As a result, the Anabaptists were widely condemned in sixteenth-century Europe, and thousands were fined, imprisoned, tortured, exiled, or executed.

In the centuries that followed, the Anabaptist movement—which had grown rapidly in the early decades through vigorous missionary activity—gradually receded. In the face of sustained persecution, many retreated to isolated hamlets in the Swiss Alps or tempered their missionary fervor in an effort to survive as an underground church. In some regions—the Palatinate, Poland, and South Russia, for example—feudal lords offered them a measure of toleration on the condition that they keep to themselves and not proselytize. As a result, the missionary zeal among the descendants of the Anabaptists—Mennonites, Hutterites, and Amish—faded. In many regions they gradually became family churches, intent on maintaining a distinctive Christian identity, but sustained largely by replicating their own communities.[44]

The missionary impulse of the Anabaptist movement, however, never disappeared entirely. In the late seventeenth century, for example, the Pietist renewal movement brought a wave of new converts into Swiss Mennonite communities. Herrnhut missionaries in the eighteenth century kept alive a spirit of outreach among some Mennonites in southwest Germany. And several Lutheran Pietist evangelists helped to spark a spiritual

---

44. Cf. N. van der Zijpp, "From Anabaptist Missionary Congregation to Mennonite Seclusion," in *Anabaptism and Mission*, ed. Wilbert R. Shenk (Scottdale, PA: Herald Press, 1984), 119–36.

revival among Mennonites in South Russia in the 1860s, giving rise to the mission-oriented Mennonite Brethren.

A similar impulse was at work in the Netherlands in the course of the nineteenth century. In 1797, members of the dominant Reformed Church established the first Dutch missionary society (Nederlandsch Zendeling Genootschap, or NZG), following the lead of British Christians who had come to regard missions as an essential component in the "civilizing" task of their expanding empire. Dutch Mennonites were active on the board of the NZG and wealthy Mennonite merchants supported its activities.

In the early 1820s, Henry Angas, representing the Baptist Missionary Society in England, traveled to the Netherlands with the goal of soliciting support among Mennonites for missions in the British Empire.[45] Thanks largely to his efforts, Dutch Mennonites—who shared with the Baptists a commitment to believers baptism—founded a branch of the Baptist Missionary Society to support its work of spreading the gospel, translating the Bible, and promoting education. Mennonites, however, soon expressed frustration with the Baptists for their narrow emphasis on doctrine as well as their focus on India. In the words of one pastor, Mennonites preferred to support missions "that are connected with the overseas possessions of our own state."[46]

Thus, in 1847, after an effort to form an auxiliary society with the NZG floundered when Mennonites refused to endorse infant baptism, a small group of Dutch Mennonite ministers, seminary professors, and business leaders—mostly

---

45. Cf. John D. Roth, "William Henry Angas Encounters the Mennonites: How Nineteenth-Century Palatine Mennonites Became Protestant," *Mennonite Quarterly Review* 94 (Oct. 2020): 421–42.

46. Alle Hoekema, *Dutch Mennonite Mission in Indonesia: Historical Essays* (Elkhart, IN: Institute of Mennonite Studies, 2001), 13.

from Amsterdam—formed the Mennonite Mission Society (Doopsgezinde Zendings Vereniging, or DZV). Initially, the new organization was understood to be a private initiative, independent of congregational or conference control. In light of the long-standing Dutch interests in the East Indies, the Mennonite Mission Society turned its primary focus to Indonesia and set about to recruit its first missionary.

PIETER JANSZ

Pieter Jansz (1820–1904), a member of the Mennonite Church in Amsterdam, had begun his career as an elementary school teacher.[47] But in 1848, after the sudden death of his young wife, Johanna, he applied to the Mennonite Mission Society and began to receive theological training at the Mennonite Seminary in Amsterdam and tutoring in Javanese geography, language, and culture at the Royal Academy in Delft. In June 1851 Jansz married Jacoba Wilhelmina Schmilau, a member of the Reformed Church. Two months later the couple embarked for Java. Neither would ever return to the Netherlands.

Soon after their arrival in Java in the fall of 1851, Pieter and Wilhelmina Jansz settled in the port city of Jepara, situated on the northern coast in the shadows of Mount Muria. For a brief time, Jansz worked as a private tutor for the children of Markar Soekias, an Armenian sugarcane plantation owner. On Sundays, Soekias compelled his workers to listen to Jansz preach, hoping that Christianity would make his labor force more compliant. Jansz quickly recognized that his listeners resented the sermons and associated his outreach with colonial

---

47. For a helpful overview of Pieter Jansz's ministry, see Alle Hoekema, "Pieter Jansz (1820–1904): First Mennonite Missionary to Java," *Mennonite Quarterly Review* 52 (Jan. 1978): 58–76.

oppression. After only a few months, he applied to the government for a license to open an elementary school in Sumbring, near Mlonggo in Central Java.

To his surprise, the license also included permission to evangelize. Jansz protested, arguing that his purpose was to start schools, not a mission, and that the government did not have the right to grant or deny Christians permission to share the gospel.[48] Yet, his protest notwithstanding, Jansz clearly was in Indonesia as a missionary. He had been sent by the Mennonite Mission Society, reported regularly to its board, and was expected to produce results in the form of a growing church.

Those results were slow in coming. On Easter Sunday, April 16, 1854, Jansz celebrated his first baptisms—one man and four women. Over the next two years, he reported nine more baptisms. But five years after Jansz's arrival, the small church he had established in Jepara numbered only twenty members. When he formally retired in 1881, his thirty years of missionary efforts in Java had resulted in a congregation in Jepara of around thirty-five baptized members, with perhaps one hundred baptisms altogether.

The reasons for his limited success were complicated. Islamic influence was very strong in the Muria region, and as we have seen, Christianity was closely associated with Dutch oppression. Moreover, in contrast to the neighboring missions, Jansz was slow to baptize, waiting until new converts had demonstrated a clear understanding of basic Christian doctrine. He also expected members to live upright ethical lives and practiced church discipline with flagrant offenders. Complicating

---

48. Jansz wanted status only as a teacher, but the government identified him as a registered missionary (which included more regulations). Hoekema, *Dutch Mennonite Mission in Indonesia*, 32.

matters further, early in his ministry Jansz ran afoul of Dutch officials when he published a Christian tract without their permission, resulting in the revocation of his formal status as a missionary. Though the incident seemed to have little direct bearing on his ongoing work,[49] Jansz recognized that if the Mennonite church was going to grow, he would need to rely heavily on the assistance of lay Javanese evangelists.

Initially, he turned to J. E. Jellesma, a Reformed missionary in East Java, for help. Jellesma sent Sem Sampir, a gifted young Javanese, to assist Jansz in creating an informal Bible school to train other lay evangelists.[50] In time, Pasrah Karso, Tresno, Petroes, and Filemon began to serve in this role, and were instrumental in helping to establish small congregations in Genang, Pulojati, Karang Gondang, and Kedungpenjalin.

In the meantime, Jansz devoted a significant amount of energy and resources to establishing several elementary schools and clinics, mostly government funded, that he administered. Teachers in these schools came primarily from the Netherlands, but also, after 1881, from Mennonite Brethren churches in South Russia who were eager to join in the global mission movement.[51]

---

49. Dutch administrators feared that the tract, titled *The Time Has Come*, would trigger Muslim reprisals. The controversy soon escalated when progressive Dutch reformers regarded the censorship as a violation of the freedom of expression promised to Dutch citizens, and the issue was eventually brought to the Dutch House of Commons for debate. Hoekema, *Dutch Mennonite Mission in Indonesia*, 32–35.

50. Jansz also had close contact with the Dutch missionary W. Hoezoo in West Java, Johannes Emde in Surabaya, and C. L. Coolen in Ngoro. Each of these missionaries, like Jellesma, were engaged in efforts to contextualize the gospel in a Javanese context. Jansz actively cultivated relations with them and eventually would play an instrumental role in creating an ecumenical association of mission workers. Sukoco and Yoder, *Way of the Gospel*, 37–39.

51. Mennonite Brethren missionaries from Russia had established a mission in Sumatra already in 1869. Hoekema, *Dutch Mennonite Mission in Indonesia*, 75–96.

KYAI IBRAHIM TUNGGUL WULUNG AND THE MODEL OF AGRICULTURAL COMMUNITIES

Without a doubt, the most significant collaboration Jansz forged in the early years at Jepara—one that was to have a decisive impact on the trajectory of the Dutch Mission—was a complicated relationship with a Javanese mystic and itinerant preacher known today as Tunggul Wulung (ca. 1800–1885).[52] Details of Tunggul Wulung's biography remain shrouded in uncertainty—a rich mixture of fact and folklore. In the popular history of Indonesia today, Ibrahim Tunggul Wulung is closely associated with the Diponegoro War in the 1820s, a nationalist uprising against the Dutch colonizers in which Kyai Ngabdoollah—as Tunggul Wulung was then known[53]—played an active role as the leader of a guerilla resistance group. After the Javanese defeat, the young revolutionary retreated to a hermitage on Mount Kelud for a period of meditation, with the goal of regathering his inner spiritual strength.

There Kyai Ngabdoollah had a vision of a famous twelfth-century Javanese general, Tunggul Wulung, who was said to have resided on Mount Kelud along with the prophet-king Joyoboyo, awaiting the return of the "Just Prince," a messianic figure whom the Javanese believed would restore justice and harmony. Shortly after this vision, Kyai Ngabdoollah encountered Christianity. In one account, he heard a voice while meditating on Mount Kelud, telling him to seek the truth from a Dutch religious leader (*pandito*). In another version, a scrap of paper containing the opening words of the Ten Commandments mysteriously appeared

---

52. For the fullest treatment of Tunggul Wulung's life, thought, and legacy, see Sukoco and Yoder, *Way of the Gospel*, 26–88.

53. Kyai is the Javanese word for "teacher" or "sage." For a time, he also went by the name Raden Mas Tondo.

Pieter Jansz worked in the same area as Tunggul Wulung for thirty years, but usually following a different vision. PHOTOGRAPH COURTESY OF THE ARCHIVES OF THE DUTCH MENNONITE MISSION (DZV), AMSTERDAM CITY ARCHIVES

under his sleeping mat. As he learned more, Kyai Ngabdoollah slowly became convinced that Jesus Christ was the long-awaited Just King, and—influenced by other Javanese Christian mystics—he began to formulate an understanding of Christianity as a collection of truths that could liberate the Javanese from the suffering brought about both by Dutch colonialism and the heavy-handed imposition of Islamic culture.

Early in 1853, Kyai Ngabdoollah changed his name to Tunggul Wulung (eventually adding Ibrahim as his Christian name) and spent some time in conversation with the Dutch Reformed missionary J. E. Jellesma, as well as with C. L. Coolen, an independent missionary in Ngoro who promoted a highly indigenized form of Javanese Christianity. Very shortly thereafter, Tunggul Wulung began his long career as an itinerant evangelist, presenting the gospel in a distinctly Javanese idiom as a "teacher of wisdom" (*guru ngelmu*). His message blended basic Christian teachings with Javanese mystical wisdom and aspects of Islam. He was highly skilled in a particular form of religious debate rich in riddles and metaphors, and often framed his teachings in the form of traditional mantras (*ngelmu*). At the heart of Tunggul Wulung's teaching was a vision of a kingdom of justice and righteousness inaugurated by the arrival of a Just Prince who would restore peace and justice to Java. Until that day, believers should form their own self-sufficient communities of righteousness. The agrarian communities he envisioned would be carved out of the wilderness in isolated settings, free from the pressure to conform to the dominant Muslim culture.

In January 1854, Tunggul Wulung came to Jepara, where Sem Sampir introduced him to Pieter Jansz. The initial encounter was not entirely positive. Jansz was suspicious of Tunggul Wulung's seemingly syncretistic blend of religious teachings, noting that his understanding of Christian doctrine seemed to be limited to the Lord's Prayer, the Ten Commandments, and the Apostles' Creed. Tunggul Wulung was equally frustrated with Jansz, who seemed to look on him as an ignorant seeker rather than a religious teacher whom local Javanese regarded as

Ibrahim Tunggul Wulung founded the indigenous Javanese Christian movement in the Muria area. This portrait, commissioned by Lawrence Yoder, was created by Inanta, a portrait artist from Semarang, on the basis of notes from missionary journals, the life story of Tunggul Wulung, and portraits of persons assumed to be his relatives. PHOTOGRAPH COURTESY OF LAWRENCE YODER

a prophet. Frustrated that Jansz refused to baptize him until he had received more instruction, Tunggul Wulung and his wife returned to Jellesma, the Reformed missionary in Mojowarno, East Java, who baptized him. Nevertheless, Tunggul Wulung agreed to collaborate with Jansz in his evangelistic work in the Muria region. When he returned to Jepara, he became a member of Jansz's church and resumed his itinerant preaching.

Almost immediately, Tunggul Wulung began to draw numerous followers in the rural regions around Mount Muria. People were attracted to his vision for creating independent Christian communities, separated from the dominant Muslim culture, removed from the urban temptations of opium use, freed from the onerous labor obligations imposed by the Dutch, and committed to preserving Javanese culture, language, and folkways.[54] Without seeking permission from either the government or Jansz, Tunggul Wulung and his followers created a clearing in the jungle close to Bondo—a site where Javanese had been slaughtered by Dutch military in the Diponegoro uprising. There they established the hamlet of Ujung Jati, the first of several Christian settlements, which Tunggul Wulung hoped would embody the virtues of the coming kingdom of the Just Prince.[55]

---

54. According to the Dutch "cultivation system," introduced in 1830, villagers were obligated to provide land rent to the government by setting aside one-fifth of their rice fields for the cultivation of export crops like sugar, coffee, and indigo, or by working in a government field for one-fifth of a year (sixty-six days) if they had no land. By contrast, residents of the agricultural communities—such as those established by Tunggul Wulung—were freed from these obligations, although the leaseholder of the land was required to pay an annual rent to the government.

55. For the modern historian, the parallels to the Anabaptist movement of the sixteenth century—which emerged in 1525 immediately after the disappointing failure of the Peasants War, was fueled by an eschatological vision of the imminent return of Christ, and found expression in visibly separated communities—are striking.

Members of the Banyutowo congregation in front of the Banyutowo church building. This congregation was originally begun by Ibrahim Tunggul Wulung. PHOTOGRAPH COURTESY OF DZV ARCHIVES, AMSTERDAM CITY ARCHIVES

During the next three decades, Tunggul Wulung traveled tirelessly throughout Java, meeting freely with independent European evangelists, debating with local Islamic leaders, and planting additional agrarian communities. By the time of his death in 1885, he had established four settlements—at Bondo, Dukuhseti, Banyutowo, and Tegalombo—with a total of some 1,100 residents. His relations with Jansz and the Mennonite Mission were generally cordial, and often even collaborative. But Tunggul Wulung maintained a clear sense that those who followed his teachings—Kristen Jawa (Javanese Christians)— remained more authentic to their Javanese culture than those neighbors led by the foreign missionaries, whom he labeled Kristen Londo (Dutch Christians).[56]

---

56. Cf. Hoekema, *Dutch Mennonite Mission in Indonesia*, 36–39; and Sukoco and Yoder, *Way of the Gospel*, 26–49.

Although he always operated at the edges of the Mennonite Mission, Tunggul Wulung's legacy for the Anabaptist-Mennonite congregations that emerged in the Muria region was profound.[57] The Mennonite Mission learned much, for example, from his effort to translate the gospel into the native idiom of rural Javanese villagers. His informal, conversational style of teaching proved to be more effective than expository sermons. But Tunggul Wulung's most significant legacy on the Mission was his vision for creating intentional agrarian communities, separated from the dominant culture, committed to principles of justice and equality.

GROWTH BY ABSORBING EXISTING CONGREGATIONS

In the early 1860s, Jansz, along with a new missionary, Nicolaas Schuurmans, established an elementary school in Jepara with a branch in Bondo, marking the first foray into what would become a significant aspect of the Mission's outreach in the Muria region. Jansz also envisioned that the Mission would improve public health by organizing several local clinics, with the dream of eventually establishing a hospital and leprosarium. Both education and medical care would become significant aspects of the Mission's work in the next fifty years.

In the meantime, Tunggul Wulung's successor, a grandson named Rustiman, was less determined to maintain his distance from the Mission. In 1886, he requested baptism, and in the following year he turned over all four agrarian settlements started by Tunggul Wulung—Bondo, Dukuhseti, Banyutowo, and Tegalombo—to the Mennonite Mission, thereby increasing

---

57. Soehadiweko Djojodihardjo, one of the most influential twentieth-century leaders of the GITJ and an active participant in Mennonite World Conference, openly acknowledged his spiritual debts to Ibrahim Tunggul Wulung.

the number of believers who related to the Mission by tenfold at a single stroke.

In the late 1860s, Pasrah Karso, a gifted Javanese convert who had served the Mission for a time as a lay evangelist, decided to establish his own Christian village—more or less along the lines of Tunggul Wulung's settlements—in Kedungpenjalin, close to Bondo. Without any funding or oversight from the Mission, the congregation that emerged there flourished, growing to 150 members by 1890. As Pasrah Karso aged, however, the congregation accepted new leadership under Johann Huebert, recently arrived from South Russia, bringing an end to nearly three decades of congregational self-reliance, while adding yet another significant number of members to the Mennonite Mission.

The oldest group of Javanese Christians in the Muria area is at Kayuapu at the southern foot of Mount Muria, not far from the city of Kudus. The original house of worship was in the form of a village house, as depicted in this old photograph, though it was constructed of bricks and plaster.
PHOTOGRAPH COURTESY OF DZV ARCHIVES, AMSTERDAM CITY ARCHIVES

A similar story unfolded in Kayuapu, a village close to the city of Kudus, where Pasrah Noeriman emerged as the leader of a strong Javanese congregation initially planted by Reformed missionaries. The congregation grew rapidly in the 1850s and 1860s, even constructing a brick church house and planting a branch congregation. But as key leaders passed away, the congregation struggled. In 1898, the congregation gave itself over to the care of the Mennonite Mission.

PIETER ANTHONIE JANSZ AND THE LEGACY OF AGRICULTURAL COMMUNITIES

The concept of agrarian settlements championed by Tunggul Wulung—in some ways analogous to the self-governing colonies Mennonites had established in South Russia—captivated Pieter Jansz's imagination. In 1874, Jansz published a booklet titled *Land Development and Evangelization in Java* in which he laid out a mission strategy based on a series of planned settlements that the missionaries would help develop on land leased from the government.[58] At the time, the Dutch Mennonite Mission Society was not interested in the concept.

In 1881, Pieter Jansz retired and moved to Salatiga, where he focused on translating the Bible into Javanese. It was Jansz's successor as head of the Mission—his son Pieter Anthonie Jansz (1853–1943)—who made agricultural settlements a central feature of the Mission's strategy, while also working to establish a host of educational and medical institutions.

In the summer of 1881 the colonial government granted P. A. Jansz a seventy-five-year lease on a three-hundred-acre tract of land close to the shore of the Java Sea that was to be the

---

58. Sukoco and Yoder, *Way of the Gospel*, 155–78.

first settlement sponsored by the Mission. The land in the new community, which the younger Jansz called Margorejo, was open to Christians and non-Christians alike, though the regulations that would structure the new village were clearly based on Christian principles. Much like the Mennonite colonies in South Russia—home to missionaries Johann Huebert, Nicolai Thiessen, and Johann Fast, who arrived in Java several years earlier—the lines between the congregational standards and settlement rules were often blurred. Residents who gambled, danced, smoked opium, imbibed hard drink, worked on the Sabbath, or kept charms and amulets could be expelled from the village. As in South Russia, land would be sublet to tenant farmers, who had heritable claims to the land they worked. Unlike the Mennonite colonies in Russia, however, ultimate authority over the settlements in Central Java was in the hands of a single individual—namely, P. A. Jansz.

At its best, the agricultural settlement in Margorejo—and a similar community founded in 1898 called Margokerto—promised its Javanese inhabitants access to land suitable for supporting a family, freedom from labor obligations, and a space to practice Christian faith removed from the pressures of the dominant Muslim culture. The model fit nicely with an Anabaptist-Mennonite view of the church as a community of believers, whose lives intersected with each other not only for worship on Sunday mornings but throughout the week as well in tangible forms of mutual aid.

At its worst, however, the settlement model advocated by the Mission was a modified form of Dutch colonialism—a sort of miniature state church that sought to "Christianize" its residents through strict moral regulations and a culture of dependence that would continue to echo well into the twentieth century.

In a crucial decision that would have long-term consequences, P. A. Jansz set aside a portion of land for the settlement's congregation as well as for the Mission itself. Over time, these church-owned properties, with the Mission serving as the land's administrator, would become a standard source of income. As a result, the emerging congregations in the Muria region did not develop the practice of tithing or a sense that their contributions were essential for the mission of the church. When the income from these lands dried up in the twentieth century and congregations attempted to introduce tithing, members reacted negatively, regarding it as a kind of tax or membership fee.

By 1885 Javanese families lived in the Margorejo community with a total population of 137 people. P. A. Jansz shifted the Mission headquarters from Jepara, oversaw the construction of a church building, and established a school in the community that quickly attracted students from the surrounding territory. In 1898, the Mission created a second settlement—Margokerto ("road to well-being")—with a similar long-term lease of a 560-acre tract of land to the northwest of Mount Muria.

At the turn of the century, the Mission supplied teachers for nearly a dozen small schools, funded by the government, associated with each of the congregations. In 1902 the newly established Conference of Missionaries opened a teacher training school in the hopes that graduates would soon be able to teach in the growing number of elementary and secondary schools it was supporting. The school operated under P. A. Jansz's supervision until 1932. The Mission also established polyclinics in Margorejo (1894) and Kedungpenjalin (1902), staffed by European doctors and nurses. And in 1915, it opened a hospital in Kelet, with a leprosarium nearby known as Donorojo ("gift of the queen"), since it was funded by a group of Dutch

The Tayu Mission Hospital, shown here before it was damaged in World War II, eventually replaced the Kelet Mission Hospital as the Central Mennonite Mission Hospital in the Muria area. PHOTOGRAPH COURTESY OF DZV ARCHIVES, AMSTERDAM CITY ARCHIVES

aristocrats in honor of Queen Wilhelmina. Later, the central hospital of the Mission shifted to Tayu, with branch hospitals and polyclinics scattered throughout the Muria region.

AN AMBIGUOUS LEGACY

By 1925 the Dutch Mission Society had been present in the Muria region of Java for nearly seventy-five years. Three generations of Mennonite missionaries—originally from the Netherlands, but soon with representatives from South Russia, Germany, and Switzerland—had devoted their lives to the mission cause. And they had much to show for their efforts. The church that they had helped nurture comprised eleven congregations and several branch congregations organized into four districts—Kedungpenjalin (Jepara), Margorejo, Kayuapu

(Kudus), and Kelet/Donorojo—with a total membership of 2,130 baptized adults and at least as many children. The elementary and secondary schools had educated hundreds of Javanese villagers, with graduates of the Teachers Training School beginning to replace Europeans as teachers and school administrators. A half dozen clinics and hospitals, along with the leprosarium at Donorojo, had immeasurably improved the physical health of many Javanese in the Muria region.

The missionaries who arrived in Java committed themselves fully to mastering Javanese or Malay and, in general, attempted to understand the nuances of Javanese culture and to treat their Javanese coworkers with respect. The agricultural settlements in Margorejo and Margokerto provided Javanese farmers a measure of economic security and freedom from the oppressive labor obligations. In 1878, the Mennonite linguist H. C. Klinkert completed the first translation of the entire Bible into Malay. A decade later, Pieter Jansz published a translation of the New Testament into Javanese; and his translation of the Old Testament soon followed in 1892. And at several key moments, the Mennonite Mission provided a home for congregations once led by Tunggul Wulung, Pasrah Karso, and Pasrah Noeriman that were in need of a broader network of support.

Yet for all the earnest—sometimes sacrificial—efforts on the part of Mennonite missionaries to embody the good news of the gospel in word and deed, the legacy of the Dutch Mission to Java remains somewhat ambiguous. In virtually every instance, the missionaries embodied the ideals of missionary practice as understood in their time. But as we will see in the following chapter, those practices, however well intended, could disguise the patterns of paternalism encouraged by the Mission that made it extremely difficult for churches in the Muria region to develop a healthy independent identity of their own. The process by which the first Javanese congregations were declared "mature"—that is, entrusted with an ordained Javanese pastor and able to function independent of Mission finances—proved to be extremely complicated. Habits of financial, spiritual, and administrative dependence, cultivated by the Mission for more than seventy-five years, were difficult to overcome.

Not until 1929 did the Conference of Missionaries ordain the first Javanese pastor; and it would take another five years before the church's young people began to receive formal training at a Bible school or seminary.[59] Nearly all the schools that the Mission helped establish were financed by the government; when government funds were in short supply, the schools generally closed. On the surface, the idea of providing congregations with plots of land seemed like a creative approach to helping them move toward financial self-sufficiency, but the missionaries struggled to turn over actual ownership of the land. When they did, the land itself became a source of intense conflict. And in the end, income generated by church properties led to a weakened sense of responsibility among members for the work of their congregations.

Although the missionaries worshiped alongside their Javanese neighbors in the small congregations in Jepara and Margorejo, Tunggul Wulung's sharp distinction between Kristen Jawa and Kristen Londo accurately reflected a painful reality—most baptized members in the Muria churches had come into the orbit of the Mennonite mission as Kristen Jawa "transfers" from congregations established by Tunggul Wulung, Pasrah Karso, and Pasrah Noeriman, or they had

59. In 1934 Soehadiweko Djojodihardjo began studies at the Higher Theological School in Batavia.

been baptized in the context of seeking land and new economic opportunities in the agricultural settlements of Margorejo and Margokerto.

None of these tensions, of course, were unique to the Mennonite Mission in Java. Cross-cultural encounters are almost always fraught with power imbalances, with consequences that are frequently unnoticed and unintended. And in many ways, the Mission pushed against the painful legacy of Dutch colonial oppression, albeit in a muted key. But when the traumatic events of the Great Depression, World War II, and the Indonesian War of Independence hit the Muria region in the 1930s and 1940s, the congregations nurtured by the Conference of Missionaries were not very well equipped to respond.

The persistence—and, ultimately, the flourishing—of Javanese Anabaptist-Mennonite churches since then is nothing short of a miracle. As we'll explore in the next three chapters, each of the three groups has followed a distinct trajectory. Today, as in the 1920s, the GITJ is largely rural, mostly Javanese, and concentrated in the Muria region; in 2018 the GITJ reported 114 congregations and a baptized membership of 45,000. The GKMI church, which emerged in the 1920s among the Chinese community in Kudus, has generally found itself at home in urban settings and has now expanded far beyond the island of Java and the Chinese character of its origin. Today, the 56 congregations in GKMI claim 18,000 baptized members. The JKI, the third and youngest of the Anabaptist-Mennonite synods, emerged out of a conscious desire to be an indigenous church, free from any economic dependency on Western missionaries or financing. Since its founding in 1985, the JKI has experienced astonishing growth, numbering more than 300 congregations, with 40,000 members.

All of these groups are thriving today, each in their own way, even as they face the perennial challenge of forging a vibrant theological and ecclesial identity in the midst of a rapidly changing cultural context. Together they offer a testimony to the power of the Holy Spirit to renew and reform the church and the remarkable ways in which the good news of the gospel can find expression in new and surprising ways.

4

The Evangelical Javanese Church

(Gereja Injili di Tanah Jawa—GITJ)

WHEN APPROACHING THE imposing GITJ church in the seaport city of Jepara, the first thing that strikes a visitor is the intricately carved woodwork decorating not only the main doors, but virtually every surface of the interior as well. Located in Central Java in the shadow of Mount Muria, Jepara is renowned throughout Indonesia for its traditional teak wood carving and fine mahogany furniture. Indeed, several of the congregation's members make their living as carvers or carpenters.

Just as quickly, however, one's eyes are drawn to a remarkable painting at the front of the sanctuary—a leaf-shaped figure, known as *Gunungan*, familiar in traditional Javanese art and theater as a representation of the world. Designed by

Harjo Suyitno, a former Muslim who is now a member of the GITJ Jepara congregation, the Gunungan depicted here has been reconceived as a symbol of the cosmic Christ (Colossians 1:15ff) in which all creation is reconciled under the authority of Jesus.[60]

Other aspects of the church—the elevated pulpit, for example, the vestments worn by its pastors, and the liturgical formality of the worship service—reflect the lingering influence of the Reformed tradition and the legacy of nearly three centuries of Dutch colonial rule. Yet the deepest history and identity of the congregation and the synod known today as the Evangelical Javanese Church (Gereja Injili di Tanah Jawa, or GITJ) reaches back to the 1850s and an unlikely fusion between the evangelistic efforts of Dutch Mennonite missionaries and an indigenous Christian renewal movement led by the Javanese mystic Tunggul Wulung.[61]

The GITJ, one of the three Indonesian synods with membership in the Mennonite World Conference, is home to more than one hundred congregations and forty-five thousand baptized members. Although the church includes a mission outreach on the island of Sumatra, most of its congregations are located in the rural farming and seaside regions of Central Java, and the identity of the synod remains firmly rooted in the Javanese language and culture of the Muria region.

---

60. "Everything Is under the Authority of Christ," MWC press release, November 25, 2019, https://mwc-cmm.org/th/node/3556.

61. Again, I am deeply indebted to the work of Sigit Heru Sukoco and Lawrence Yoder for much of the detail in this chapter. Sigit Heru Sukoco and Lawrence M. Yoder, *The Way of the Gospel in the World of Java: A History of the Muria Javanese Mennonite Church (GITJ)* (Goshen, IN: Institute for the Study of Global Anabaptism, 2020).

Exterior doors to the GITJ Jepara church building, showing the exquisite wood carving for which the city is famous. PHOTOGRAPH COURTESY OF DANIEL TALENTA

The *Gunungan* image, typical in traditional Javanese art, has been reconceived in the GITJ Jepara church as a Christian representation of the world, rich in biblical imagery. PHOTOGRAPH COURTESY OF DANIEL TALENTA

A COMPLICATED BIRTH

Dating the birth of the church that was to become the GITJ is a bit tricky. One possibility would be April 16, 1854, the day that Dutch Mennonite missionary Pieter Jansz, who had arrived in Java several years earlier, baptized the first five Javanese converts as the core of a new congregation he hoped to start in Jepara. However, as we saw in chapter 3, the church Jansz planted struggled mightily in the decades that followed, adding only a handful of new believers each year. Instead, the key figures in the growth of the church were other Javanese spiritual leaders like Tunggul Wulung, Pasrah Karso, and Pasrah Noeriman. And it was Tunggul Wulung's vision of an agricultural community—the first of which he established in 1856—that profoundly shaped the direction of the emerging church in the first century of its existence.[62]

The Margorejo congregation's decision on June 27, 1928, to name Roeben Martoredjo as its pastor—the first time that a Javanese congregation selected its own leader—suggests yet another plausible date for the birth of the GITJ synod. Or perhaps the key moment was the Mennonite Mission's declaration on March 4, 1929, of the "maturity" of Margorejo congregation; or the formal ordination of Roeben Martoredjo that took place several months later that same year in August. Still another consideration would be the meeting on May 29, 1940, when representatives of the twelve congregations associated with the Mennonite Mission gathered in Kelet to create the synod that would eventually be known as the GITJ.

---

62. The first agricultural community was a hamlet created close to Margokerto called Ujung Jati.

Locating the beginning of a church in terms of a single date is a somewhat arbitrary exercise, of course. But as a symbol of spiritual empowerment and independence, the ordination of Roeben Martoredjo on August 12, 1929, seems like a worthy moment to commemorate. Coming seventy-five years after the first baptisms in the Muria region, the ordination marked a crucial step in the prolonged process by which the Muria Javanese Church became a self-standing or "mature" ecclesial body.

In retrospect, it seems astonishing that it took nearly three generations of mission work in Central Java before the first Javanese leader was empowered with the authority to carry out such basic rituals as baptism and communion, and close to ninety years before the Muria Javanese Church would develop an organizational structure entrusted with control over its own financial assets, administrative organization, and theological identity. That this final move toward independence would happen precisely at a time of global economic crisis, followed by a world war and the Japanese occupation of Indonesia, made the transition all the more difficult.

In some ways, the survival of the GITJ is a kind of a miracle. That it persists as a healthy, thriving church today is a testimony to God's grace, the resilience of its members, and the persistent presence of the Holy Spirit.

FIRST STEPS TOWARD "MATURITY"

At the beginning of the twentieth century, the Dutch Mennonite Mission Society in the Netherlands could report that twelve congregations had been established in Java, most of them associated with several small branch outposts, and numbering approximately four thousand baptized members. In 1900, the Mennonite missionaries in Java organized their

Teacher Bedja Siswosoewoto (left) with his class in the Margorejo Teacher Training School in Margorejo. PHOTOGRAPH COURTESY OF DZV ARCHIVES, AMSTERDAM CITY ARCHIVES

own Conference of Missionaries that reported to the Mission Society, but exercised firm control of virtually every aspect of those twelve congregations.[63] The Conference of Missionaries, for example, oversaw the work of the lay "gospel teachers" assigned to each of the congregations and paid them a small salary. They also administered several elementary and intermediate schools, negotiating with the government, which covered most of the costs. It supported several clinics, the hospital at Tayu, a leprosarium at Donorojo, and the Teacher Training School at Margorejo. And, not least, the Conference of Missionaries managed the administration of the agricultural communities at Margorejo and Margokerto and controlled the significant revenue that they generated.

---

63. At the same time, virtually all the revenue needed to fund the work of the Mission—including schools, medical facilities, lay evangelists, and the maintenance of the missionaries themselves—came from the Mission Society in Amsterdam or the Dutch colonial government, a dynamic that easily created conflict over questions of authority and control.

In 1910 the Conference of Missionaries took a first small step toward granting the Javanese congregations greater independence by appointing representatives or intermediaries in several of the larger congregations such as Kedungpenjalin and Margorejo, giving them the task of communicating information from the Mission to the local congregations. By 1917 these representatives had evolved into a kind of church council that was charged, among other things, with the challenge of helping their congregations move toward financial self-sufficiency, or "maturity."

Progress in this area, however, remained slow. Until this point, all the salaries for the Javanese evangelists and gospel teachers had been funded by the Dutch Mennonite Mission Society, supplemented by money generated by the agricultural communities. The concept of tithing—or the principle of self-sufficiency—had never been part of the missionary teaching. Not surprisingly, when mission workers and, later, Javanese church leaders attempted to introduce the concept, congregational members, most of whom were poor fishermen or subsistence farmers, regarded it as an unwelcome tax or a newly imposed membership fee.

In 1928, Hermann Schmitt, a young missionary from Germany, took the principle of self-sufficiency one step further when he proposed to the local Conference of Missionaries that Javanese pastors (*pamomong*) be appointed for the large congregations at Margorejo, Kedungpenjalin, and Kayuapu, and then ordained with the authority to baptize and officiate at communion. Somewhat reluctantly, the Mission agreed, announcing that they would start with Margorejo, provided that the congregation meet the following conditions: "1) provide for their own financial needs; 2) operate their own congregational

Roeben Martoredjo, seated here with his wife (name unknown), was the first Javanese person to be ordained as a minister in the Muria Javanese Church. The ordination occurred on August 12, 1929.
PHOTOGRAPH COURTESY OF DZV ARCHIVES, AMSTERDAM CITY ARCHIVES

organization; 3) move forward on their own strength and initiative; and 4) be prepared to sacrifice."[64]

The Conference of Missionaries then identified two pastoral candidates whom they deemed worthy of ordination and asked the congregation to make the final selection. On June 27, 1928, the Margorejo church council chose Roeben Martoredjo and made plans to ordain him the following week. When the Mennonite Mission Society board in Amsterdam heard the news, however, its members were deeply upset that the local Mission had moved forward with these decisions without their explicit permission. As a consequence, Roeben Martoredjo's ordination and installation as the first Javanese pastor in the Muria church did not take place until August 12, 1929, more than a year later.

---

64. Sukoco and Yoder, *Way of the Gospel*, 245.

Even then, Margorejo's "independence" was understood by the missionaries to be only for a provisional five-year trial period, during which "there must be evidence that Margorejo can really stand on its own."[65] The assets and financial affairs of the congregation would be turned over "only gradually" during the same five-year period. Moreover, when, in 1933, the mission board in Amsterdam finally granted the congregation control over its own finances, the Margorejo agricultural community—a primary source of income for both the congregation and the Mission—remained firmly in the hands of the missionaries.

In the meantime, the economic crisis unleashed by the Great Depression had also reached Indonesia, resulting in the closure of the Margorejo Teacher Training School in 1932. With the school closed, congregations had even fewer opportunities to train future teachers, pastors, and church leaders, making the move toward independence all the more difficult.

Not until 1937—eighty-five years after the first baptisms—did a handful of Javanese young people begin to pursue formal theological education beyond the basic courses that had been offered at the Teacher Training School. In that year, two young church members, Suwignyo Harsosoedirdjo and I. S. Siswojo, enrolled in the Bale Wiyoto Theology School in Malang, while Soehadiweko Djojodihardjo, a promising young leader from Pati, received a scholarship to attend the Higher Theological School in Batavia.

These investments in higher education would prove to be profoundly important. In subsequent years, both Harsosoedirdjo and Siswojo would play key ministerial and administrative roles in the GITJ synod. And Djojodihardjo would soon emerge as

---

65. Sukoco and Yoder, 247.

a highly influential leader in the Javanese church, one of the few Javanese leaders of his generation to learn Dutch and to develop extensive contacts with Anabaptist-Mennonite leaders in other parts of the world. Although Djojodihardjo was to play a powerful—largely positive—role in shaping the identity of the GITJ in the coming decades, because none of his peers enjoyed a similar level of education, his authority in the GITJ church in decades to come was virtually unrivaled.

By the early 1940s, the Muria Javanese Church consisted of twelve congregations and twenty-nine branch congregations. The congregations were divided into three districts—Kudus, Kedungpenjalin, and Kelet—with a missionary assigned to each district to provide ongoing oversight. Each of the congregations received a small measure of financial support for lay gospel teachers; only one church, Margorejo, had an ordained pastor. The Mission also continued to support a network of schools—eighteen three-year elementary schools and four two-year middle schools—as well as a cluster of medical facilities.

For the first time, the Mission began to ask what the organizational structure of the Javanese church might look like independent of the administrative oversight it had long provided. Since Dutch, German, Swiss, and Russian Mennonite missionaries had always generated the initiative and funding for larger projects such as education, healthcare, and other social services, the congregations had little experience in self-administration or in collaborating with each other in sharing resources or joint decisions. In 1935, Hermann Schmitt, drawing on the model of the Mennonite church in the Netherlands, proposed the creation of a conference that would unite the congregations under a common administrative umbrella. When that plan met with resistance from local congregational leaders, Schmitt shifted toward a church polity modeled on the German Mennonite churches that granted much greater autonomy to individual congregations.

The result was a somewhat confusing synodal structure that was ultimately unclear about the actual authority of the synod vis-à-vis the congregations. Further complicating the new model was the Mission's continued administration of the landholdings of the agricultural settlements, along with a large number of schools and hospitals. In the words of historians Sigit Heru Sukoco and Lawrence Yoder, "The mission simply could not conceive of Indonesian churches and their associated ministries apart from the Dutch Mennonite Mission and the Conference of Missionaries. The federal conference organization that they proposed could not possibly provide for what the churches, soon to become independent entities, would have to face."[66]

Further adding to the confusion was the fact that the plan for independence did not address a host of complex legal questions, including the incorporation of church bodies, governmental recognition of the newly created synod, ownership of congregational properties, and the long-term legal status of the schools, clinics, and hospitals. "If all these preparations for independence were only a kind of stage play," write Sukoco and Yoder, "it is not surprising that they did not attract much interest on the part of the Javanese Indonesian members or church leaders."[67]

THE END OF THE COLONIAL ERA: WORLD WAR II AND INDONESIAN INDEPENDENCE

At precisely this precarious moment of transition toward greater independence, events unfolding thousands of miles away brought about an abrupt end to the Mennonite Mission in

66. Sukoco and Yoder, 253.
67. Sukoco and Yoder, 254.

Indonesia and confronted the Muria Javanese congregations with a series of existential challenges.

In the fall of 1939, German armies attacked and occupied most of Poland; several months later, the blitzkrieg continued the German advance into Denmark and Norway. And on May 10, 1940, Hitler's armies, supported by aerial attacks from the Luftwaffe, invaded the Netherlands. The German occupation effectively severed all connections between the Netherlands and its colonies in the East Indies. For the Muria Javanese Church, this meant a sudden end to most of the financial and administrative support from the local Mission and the Mennonite Mission Society in Amsterdam.

Three weeks later, on May 30, 1940, the Mennonite Mission Society formally recognized the "Fellowship of Gospel-Way Christian Congregations in the Area of Pati, Kudus, and Jepara Counties" (Patoenggilan Pasamoewan Kristen Tata Indjil ing Karesidenan Pati, Koedoes, lan Djepara) as an independent, self-sufficient church body.[68] Most of the positions in the newly created synod were held by Javanese church members. Yet perhaps to no one's surprise, Daniel Amstutz, a missionary from Switzerland who had remained in Java, emerged as the chairperson of the new organization, and Dr. Karl Gramberg as the assistant chairperson. The first act of the synod was to send a delegation to each of the congregations—Kedungpenjalin, Banyutowo, Margorejo, Pati, Kudus,

---

68. The precise language to describe the new organization is a bit confusing, giving rise to a protracted debate in the years that followed over the exact nature and scope of its authority. Technically, *patunggilan pasamuwan* means a "church fellowship" or "association" or "union." But the organization soon referred to its gatherings as "synods," which—if one looks to the Reformed model—points to a somewhat stronger central authority than might be suggested by words like *association* and *fellowship*.

Kayuapu, Tayu, Donorojo, Bandungharjo, Kelet, Margokerto, and Bondo—to assess the status of local leadership and the finances of the congregation. The group also quickly moved to ordain five gospel teachers as credentialed ministers.

At the first general assembly, held the following year (May 27–28, 1941), a debate ensued over the statement of faith that Amstutz had drafted for the synodal constitution. Among various affirmations of orthodox Christian beliefs, Amstutz had also included several distinctive Anabaptist-Mennonite motifs such as baptism on confession of faith, a rejection of the oath and military service, and a commitment to nonresistance in one's personal life. These latter points gave rise to a significant debate, especially among the young people.

Immediately following the German occupation of the Netherlands in the spring of 1940, Indonesians throughout the country joined in a nationalist movement for Indonesian independence. In the context of that struggle, led largely by Indonesia's Islamic majority, Christianity continued to be close-ly associated with Dutch colonial rule, something the young people in the Muria Javanese Church deeply resented. If the newly created synod was now going to reject participation in the armed struggle for Indonesian independence, most of the youth were not likely to continue their involvement in the church. After an intense conversation, participants at the as-sembly agreed to drop the principle of nonresistance from the shared statement of faith. In response, Amstutz resigned.

By the spring of 1942 the Imperial Japanese Army occu-pied Indonesia as part of Japan's larger advance throughout Southeast Asia. Initially, most Javanese greeted the Japanese as liberators. But in the political vacuum created by the Dutch retreat, a radical Muslim group known as Ansor emerged in the Muria region and directed a wave of destruction and terror against Christians and ethnic Chinese. On Sunday, March 8, 1942, Ansor mobs seized church leaders from Tayu at gunpoint and took them to the town of Bulumanis, where, under threat of torture and execution, the leaders were forced to deny their faith and repeat Muslim prayers.

Further attacks in the coming days on the leprosarium at Donorojo and the hospital at Tayu left several dead, and resulted in significant damage to the hospital and neighboring church. Other Ansor groups destroyed church buildings at Tegalombo and Margorejo and forced the humiliated church leaders to publicly repeat Muslim confessions. In Kelet, congregation members successfully organized an armed defense against the mob; in Margokerto, by contrast, panicked members of the community joined in the plunder of the congregation's property.[69]

Within a few weeks, Japanese authorities put an end to the violence, but the physical suffering and material damage—along with the humiliation suffered by their leaders—left a deep wound in the Muria Javanese Church, which was already struggling with internal challenges of leadership and identity. In the fall of 1942 the synod convened at Juana Hospital, this time with only eight congregations represented. At the gathering, Amstutz and Gramberg formally turned over the titles of all Mission properties to Javanese leaders, a largely symbolic gesture since by then the schools and hospitals were either destroyed or under Japanese control.[70] A second synod assembly, held in Pati the following spring (April 1943), reorganized the

69. Sukoco and Yoder, *Way of the Gospel*, 287–88.

70. As German and Swiss citizens, respectively, Gramberg and Amstutz were spared the reprisals that the Dutch missionaries faced.

congregations into districts in an effort to provide a stronger framework for mutual aid. Meanwhile, the Japanese occupying army forcibly recruited and relocated millions of Javanese laborers to work in armaments factories throughout Southeast Asia. An estimated four million people died in the Dutch East Indies because of famine and forced labor during the three years of Japanese occupation.[71]

Two months after the Japanese defeat in August 1945, church leaders convened General Synod Meeting III (October 1945) to begin the process of rebuilding the Muria Javanese Church. At the gathering a major conflict again erupted between older leaders and a group of energized youth who were eager for the church to engage in politics, and especially in the struggle for Indonesian national liberation against the Dutch, who were now renewing their colonial claims over the archipelago. In an attempt at compromise, representatives agreed that the youth would be free to participate in political activities, including the various guerrilla movements that were forming to resist Dutch rule. The older generation would support the nationalist movement with prayer. The synod also voted to remove the language of *Tata Injil* (or "gospel way") from its name to become simply the Fellowship of Christian Congregations in the Muria Area.[72] Additionally, it sought to strengthen the authority of the synod structure by claiming ownership of the agricultural properties, promoting theological training for church leaders, and creating a shared liturgy to be used by all the congregations.

---

71. Among those who died were some thirty thousand European civilians. John W. Dower, *War without Mercy: Race and Power in the Pacific War* (New York: Pantheon, 1986), 296.
72. Sukoco and Yoder, *Way of the Gospel*, 301.

RESHAPING CHURCH IDENTITY IN POSTCOLONIAL INDONESIA

Who is our family of faith?

In June 1949, as the Indonesian Wars of Liberation were coming to an end, synod leaders met again to reflect on the future identity of the church. The meeting marked a crucial moment in the history of the Muria Javanese Church. The church had endured enormous uncertainty and suffering, marked by mob violence, an occupying army, and a long revolutionary struggle that finally resulted in the end of Dutch colonial rule. Since the outbreak of the war, membership in the Muria Javanese Church had declined by half (from four thousand to two thousand). Its legal status was in limbo, and ownership of properties that once belonged to the Mission—including the large agricultural communities and other congregationally owned land that the Japanese had appropriated—now reverted to the new Indonesian government.

A strong ecumenical current emerged among the Christian churches in Java, all of which had been weakened by the war.[73] And church leaders remained uncertain about the future theological identity of the Muria Javanese synod. At the 1949 gathering, representatives of the Central Java Christian Church, a Reformed synod, made a strong argument that the Muria Javanese Church should merge with their group. As Soehadiweko Djojodihardjo, a rising leader in the Muria Javanese Church, openly acknowledged, "It is very clear that the churches of the Muria area no longer accept basic Mennonite teachings because we have gone to war and have taken oaths. We honestly confess that the Muria area church no longer

---

73. For more on the strong ecumenical impulses among Javanese Christians immediately following the war, see Jan Sihar Aritonang and Karel Steenbrink, eds., *A History of Christianity in Indonesia* (Leiden: Brill, 2008), 685–86.

maintains this particular identity."[74] But when Daniel Amstutz, the Swiss Mennonite missionary who had ardently advocated for nonresistance at an earlier synod meeting, asked the group to remain in fellowship with the Anabaptist-Mennonite tradition despite their ambivalence about the gospel of peace, the synod agreed.

In the coming years church leaders would turn their attention to the enormous task of rebuilding their congregations, sorting out the nature of synodal authority, and restoring fraternal relationships with the Dutch Mennonites and other Anabaptist-Mennonite groups in Europe and North America.

Remarkably, the second half of the twentieth century witnessed a period of new vitality and growth as the Muria Javanese Church slowly flourished in the new context of Indonesian independence. Congregational resiliency, new collaborations with international partners, and the emergence of strong central leadership—especially the dynamic activity of Soehadiweko Djojodihardjo—all contributed to the recovery and growth of what would eventually become the Gereja Injili di Tanah Jawa.

New leadership: Soehadiweko Djojodihardjo
Among the various leaders who contributed most to the consolidation of the Muria Javanese Church in the decades after the war, the name Soehadiweko Djojodihardjo (1918–1988) looms large. The son of an influential pastor in the Pati congregation, Djojodihardjo attended the Jakarta Theological Seminary, where he learned Dutch and was exposed to a broader ecumenical world. During the Wars of Liberation, Djojodihardjo made a name for himself as a fiery organizer among the youth in the

---

74. Sukoco and Yoder, *Way of the Gospel*, 305.

armed struggle against the Dutch. In the spring of 1949 he succeeded his father as both pastor in Pati and the vice chair of the new synod, and immediately set out to reorganize the congregations into districts. When the synod chair was unable to attend the June 1949 synod meeting, Djojodihardjo stepped in.

For the next four decades Pak Djojo, as he was known, would dominate the work of the synod. Along the way, Djojodihardjo served on virtually every church-related board, created a host of new institutions, moved the congregations toward greater self-sufficiency, and represented the synod to numerous outside entities such as Mennonite Central Committee, the newly formed Dutch Mennonite Mission Council (Doopsgezinde Zendingsraad), the European Mennonite Evangelism Committee (Europäisches Mennonitisches Evangelisations Komitee, or EMEK), and Mennonite World Conference.

During his tenure as chair of the synod, Djojodihardjo successfully attracted new sources of funding, especially from European and North American Mennonites. EMEK, for example, supported the salaries of pastors and gospel teachers; MCC contributed to buildings, vehicles, and meeting expenses; and both overseas partners helped to rebuild and staff the Tayu hospital and to establish the Akademi Kristen Wiyata Wacana in Pati—a Bible school to train future church leaders. With Djojodihardjo's encouragement, the GITJ joined the Mennonite World Conference in 1951, where he became a regular speaker at subsequent global assemblies. Individual Mennonites in Europe and North America sponsored scholarships for children attending primary schools organized under the Christian Education Foundation (BOPKRI).

Some congregations—especially Margorejo and Margokerto —had regained access to agricultural lands previously owned

Traditional Javanese architecture in the Margorejo agrarian community, which still functions today as a largely Christian agricultural settlement.
PHOTOGRAPH COURTESY OF DANIEL TALENTA

by the congregations and were relatively self-sufficient thanks to the revenue these properties generated. Most, however, had very little land and no established patterns of self-support, and were especially vulnerable in times of broader economic crises. In an effort to address this, the GITJ's Diaconal Service Body helped to channel resources to those suffering from natural disasters, and the synod created an Economic Development Commission to support local entrepreneurial ventures aimed at economic self-sufficiency by channeling assistance from MCC and EMEK. The program funded a host of economic development projects—water pumps, vehicles, fishing boats, sewing machines, rice hullers, a citrus orchard, pigs, cows, chickens, goats, coconuts, and even a photography studio. Unfortunately, however, most of these projects failed to translate into sustainable incomes for Javanese church members.[75]

---

75. In 1972 this organization transformed into YAKEM, an agency with its own staff that engaged larger-scale projects, mostly funded by MCC and EKEM. Unfortunately, the vision did not produce much fruit.

The expanded role of MCC and EMEK in the 1960s and 1970s, however, proved to be a complicated gift to the Javanese churches. Clearly, the financial resources provided by these organizations were deeply welcomed by congregations in dire need of financial, social, medical, and educational support. The relationships also helped to deepen connections between members of the GITJ church and a broad network of brothers and sisters in the global church. But these new forms of dependency also came at a cost. "Unfortunately," writes historian Adhi Dharma, "the hoped for strong economic foundation that would contribute to the independence of the church could not be created. . . . Dependence on aid from the mission organizations had continued for so long and was so strong that it was very difficult to awaken a consciousness of independence in economic matters."[76]

To be sure, Djojodihardjo and other synod leaders searched for ways for GITJ congregations and the synod to become more self-sufficient. In the early 1970s, when both MCC and EMEK announced that they would be significantly reducing their financial support, Djojodihardjo and others promoted the One Rupiah Movement—an effort to persuade members to contribute one rupiah a month to the church. Although that initiative failed, some congregations did successfully raise funds needed to build new churches, and the synod developed a plan to support theology students and evangelists.

As these institutions flourished, the GITJ grew rapidly. In 1969, the church numbered 18,500 baptized members, with another 25,000 attending as children or unbaptized

---

76. Adhi Dharma, "The Mennonite Churches of Indonesia," in *Churches Engage Asian Traditions: A Global Mennonite History*, ed. John A. Lapp and C. Arnold Snyder (Intercourse, PA: Good Books, 2011), 73–104.

participants.[77] Part of this precipitous growth can be attributed to the violent riots that began on September 30, 1965 (commonly referred to in Indonesia as G-30-S) targeting communists and ethnic Chinese. In the immediate aftermath of the riots, thousands of people joined Christian churches, including the GITJ, to avoid the accusation of being communists.

Djojodihardjo's strong—at times, authoritarian—leadership style enabled the GITJ church to find its feet in the difficult years after the war. But it also evoked sharp criticism, especially from the youth. After an unsuccessful attempt to dislodge his hold on the synod while he was attending the MWC global assembly in 1967, however, Djojodihardjo continued to play a central role in the GITJ for nearly twenty more years.

When Djojodihardjo finally did step down from his multiple positions in the mid-1980s, the church struggled once again to break free from patterns of passivity and dependency cultivated by his leadership style. In the vacuum created by his absence and the withdrawal of MCC and EMEK financial support, the GITJ church struggled mightily in the 1980s and 1990s with internal conflicts over control of church properties, synod finances, and the future of its medical and educational institutions, which were facing stricter government regulations and increased competition from Islamic counterparts. In the late 1980s, synod meetings were frequently marked by debate and mutual accusations. Between 1990 and 1995 the synod did not convene at all; when it attempted to resume its meetings in the fall of 1996, most of the congregations refused to attend, forming instead a competing body that gained the support of the government.

---

77. Sukoco and Yoder, *Way of the Gospel*, 314. By 1972, GITJ had grown to include twenty-three congregations (with 119 worship groups).

In November 2000, a mediation process begun in 1998—
initiated by MCC and the Dutch Mission Council,[78] and fa-
cilitated by Lawrence Yoder—culminated with a service of
reconciliation.[79]

"NOT THE BUILDING BUT THE PEOPLE"

In the years since then, GITJ church leaders have worked tirelessly to revive dormant programs and restore confidence in synod
leadership. In August 2003, the church successfully reopened the
Wiyata Wacana Bible School in Pati. The GITJ has also drawn
increasingly on the gifts of women. Already in 1965 the GITJ
Pati congregation took a bold step when it ordained Esther
Soesanto Harso-Andries as the synod's first female pastor.[80] By
2015, 94 percent of GITJ members reported that their congregation "allows men and women to have equal ministry roles."[81]
Although the synod remains predominantly Javanese, today
nearly three-quarters of GITJ congregations include people of
different races and ethnicities, and the synod has supported an
outreach to the island of Sumatra. Other aspects of synod reflect
a deep continuity with the past. The 2015 survey, for example, re-
vealed that the GITJ remains overwhelmingly rural—91 percent

---

78. The Dutch Mission Council (Doopsgezinde Zendingsraad) was formed in
1957 when the Dutch Mennonite Mission Society became a formal entity within
the Dutch Mennonite Church (Algemene Doopsgezinde Sociëteit).

79. Dharma, "The Mennonite Churches of Indonesia," 70–71; Stefanus Christian
Haryono, "Mennonite History and Identity in Indonesia," *Mission Focus: Annual
Review* 9 (2001): 69.

80. Esther Soesanto Harso-Andries also served as the director of the Teacher Training School in Pati.

81. Conrad Kanagy, Elizabeth Miller, and John D. Roth, *Global Anabaptist Profile: Belief and Practice in 24 Mennonite World Conference Churches* (Goshen, IN:
Institute for the Study of Global Anabaptism, 2017). The detailed results from the
GITJ survey, presented by Mohamad Ichsanudin Zubaedi, are available in unpublished form.

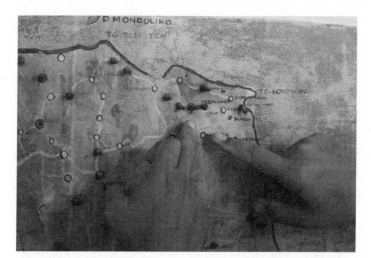

Map of North Central Java showing the location of GITJ congregations in the Muria region. The map is displayed on the campus of the GITJ Synod offices and Wiyata Wacana Theological College in Pati. PHOTOGRAPH COURTESY OF DANIEL TALENTA

of its members live in villages or small towns, mostly in the Muria region. And even though most of its members are literate, only 45 percent have graduated from high school.[82]

As it looks to the future, one of the GITJ church's biggest challenges—and one of its most impressive forms of witness—has been negotiating relationships with its Muslim neighbors in the Muria region. Here, GITJ churches are finding a remarkable balance between active evangelism and sensitive accommodation.

Shortly after Easter in 2010, for example, a group of Muslims came to the church compound of the rural GITJ congregation

---

82. Kanagy, Miller, and Roth. Another interesting finding from the survey: Although two-thirds of GITJ congregations include members who serve in the military and nearly half agree that Christians may participate in war, 92 percent agree that their congregation "teaches its members to reject violence."

where Adi Walujo served as pastor.[83] The group showed him a legal document, blocked the door of the church, and informed him that the congregation would no longer have access to the building. So the congregation began to meet in the yard outside the church, using umbrellas and plastic sheets during the rainy season. "The church," Adi Walujo said, "is not a building but the people who believe in God personally. We meet together, we worship Jesus Christ as God, and we serve him. We can still worship outside on the ground instead of in the building."

Efforts by Adi and other church leaders to learn why the building had been closed proved fruitless. But then something surprising happened. Situated on the church property was a well that supplied water for the community, the vast majority of whom are Muslim. After some discussion, the congregation, despite having been barred from entering their own church house, agreed to allow the community to continue using the well.

Shortly after Christmas, eight months after the church was closed, the Muslim community leader came to Adi Walujo to apologize. "Brother," he said, "we realize that you are good people, that you are a part of the community. Although we closed your church, the water from your well still gives life to our people in the community." In fact, the Muslim community even allowed the congregation to put a cross on the church building, something that would never have been possible before the encounter.

"Maybe people think persecution is always negative," Adi Walujo reflected. "But for us we learned how to depend on God

---

83. For the full interview in which Adi Walujo relates the story, see "Adi Walujo, Indonesia," Bearing Witness, February 17, 2016, https://martyrstories.org/adi-walujo/.

while our church was closed. We grew spiritually. . . . And God opened the door for us to have our church building again!" He continued, "We are a peace church, but that doesn't mean we have to just be quiet. We have to be an active part of the community and to show others the meaning of love—the impact of the love that we feel in our lives."

Danang Kristiawan, co-pastor of GITJ Jepara, has also actively pursued peaceable relations with the local Muslim community. "The mission of the church," writes Danang, "is to present God's love and promote peace in the world, to reconcile among the different people both in the church and in society." In 2009, Danang began a peace initiative that focused especially on art and music, because "art is the universal language of humanity."[84] The worship service celebrating his ordination included a pastor from the local charismatic church who played the piano, a dancer from the Sufi community, and a violinist from a prominent local Islamic organization. Later, at a large Muslim gathering, organizers spontaneously called Danang to the stage to offer a greeting from the Christian community. The text he shared came from 1 John 4:4-8—because God has loved us, we are called to love each other.

Today it would not be at all uncommon for anyone driving through the countryside in the region around Mount Muria to come across a modest church bearing the GITJ name and logo. Many of these rural congregations have a long and rich

---

84. Danang Kristiawan, "All Is about Love: Sharing of Interfaith Relations between the Javanese Mennonite Church and Javanese Islamic Sufi in Indonesia," unpublished paper presented at the Global Mennonite Peacebuilding Conference and Festival, Conrad Grebel University College, Waterloo, Ontario, Canada (June 9–12, 2016). In 2012 and 2014 GITJ Jepara celebrated the International Day of Peace and invited leaders from Islamic, Buddhist, Hindu, and indigenous religions to share their commitments to peace.

history, with roots reaching back well into the nineteenth century. Their presence in the Javanese landscape today testifies to the resilience of ordinary GITJ church members and the enduring gift of the Holy Spirit.

5

The Muria Christian Church of Indonesia

(Gereja Kristen Muria Indonesia—GKMI)

O N SEPTEMBER 27, 1925, Tee Siem Tat, a Chinese businessman from the Central Javanese city of Kudus, appeared at the town's local notary to formally register a congregation he had recently helped start. Five years earlier, on December 6, 1920, Tee Siem Tat had been baptized—along with twenty-four others he had helped bring to faith—by representatives of the Dutch Mennonite Mission, marking the birth of a new Christian movement in the Muria region.

Now, five years later, the congregation had prepared its own constitution, identifying Tan King Ien, Tee's son-in-law, as the chair of the congregation and Tee Siem Tat as its pastor. The following spring, the congregation applied to the Dutch East Indies government to be recognized as a legally incorporated body. On February 3, 1927, these actions, both undertaken without the knowledge of the Mennonite Mission, resulted in the creation of a new church, registered by the Dutch name of Chineesche Doopsgezinde Christengemeente (Chinese Mennonite Christian Church).

Although the roots of the GITJ, or Muria Javanese Church, with its close ties to the Dutch Mennonite Mission Society, go back to the middle of the nineteenth century, some historians have suggested that this small congregation in Kudus was actually the "first organized non-Western Mennonite church in the world." Under the leadership of Tee Siem Tat the congregation would eventually become the core of a flourishing group of churches known today as the Muria Christian Church of Indonesia (Gereja Kristen Muria Indonesia, or GKMI).[85]

Three significant characteristics distinguished the early history of the GKMI synod from its GITJ counterpart. First, in the early years of its history, GKMI members came predominantly from the Chinese community—some were longtime residents of Java; others were recent immigrants from the Chinese mainland. As a natural consequence, GKMI members initially used Chinese in their worship services rather than Javanese, and the synod became closely identified with the broader Chinese community of Muria.

Second, as the name selected by the Kudus congregation suggests, the GKMI had close connections to the Dutch Mennonite Mission, but Tee Siem Tat's decision to incorporate the group without seeking permission from missionary leaders

---

85. The main outlines of this chapter rely heavily on two sources: Lawrence M. Yoder, *The Muria Story: A History of the Chinese Mennonite Churches of Indonesia* (Kitchener, ON: Pandora Press, 2006); and Adhi Dharma, "The Mennonite Churches of Indonesia," in *Churches Engage Asian Traditions: A Global Mennonite History*, ed. John A. Lapp and C. Arnold Snyder (Intercourse, PA: Good Books, 2011), 73–104. Quotation in this paragraph from Yoder, *Muria Story*, 7.

makes it clear that the GKMI understood itself to be fully capable of making its own independent decisions as an equal partner with the Mission.

Finally, in contrast to the emerging GITJ, which was overwhelmingly rural in its membership, the group that formed around the leadership of Tee Siem Tat tended to be urban, and its members were, on average, somewhat wealthier and better educated than their GITJ counterparts. Over time, all of these distinctions became much less pronounced. But in the early years of the church, these differences meant that the GKMI would develop a quite different identity from that of the GITJ.

ETHNIC CHINESE COMMUNITIES IN JAVA

Like the Muria Javanese Church, the early history of the movement that evolved into the GKMI synod was closely associated with the Dutch Mennonite Mission in the Muria region. But the relationship was complicated, characterized by an ongoing struggle over identity and control. A key factor in that struggle was the predominantly Chinese character of the GKMI movement.

Relations in Java between Javanese and ethnic Chinese were complicated. Like Jewish communities of medieval Europe, the Chinese community maintained a distinctive identity. This was partly a function of language. Although many Chinese spoke Javanese, they were generally more comfortable speaking Chinese or Malay, a variant of Bahasa common in Malaysia. As a religious minority—predominantly Confucian—they celebrated traditional Chinese religious and cultural events in public ways that could prove irritating to Islamic leaders. They also filled a needed, albeit often resented, role in the local economy as entrepreneurial merchants, shopkeepers, factory owners, and moneylenders. And they were often assumed to be complicit with Dutch colonial rule, acting as intermediaries between Dutch administrators and local Javanese.

There were many exceptions to these stereotypes, of course. Within the Chinese community there were sharp differences between those of Chinese descent (*kiauwseng*)—who spoke Javanese and were more fully acculturated—and more recent immigrants (*hoakiao*) who fully embraced their Chinese identity. Moreover, for long stretches of time, relations between ethnic Chinese and their Javanese neighbors could be very congenial. But undercurrents of hostility and resentment stubbornly persisted, and would find expression in repeated paroxysms of violence directed against the Chinese community throughout the twentieth century.

Soon after his arrival in 1851, Pieter Jansz had attempted to reach out to the minority Chinese community in Jepara. Indeed, several of the earliest members of the church were ethnic Chinese. In 1873, H. C. Klinkert, a Dutch colleague in the Mennonite Mission, translated the Bible into Malay, the language spoken by many ethnic Chinese who had settled in the Indonesian islands. In 1899 the Reformed Dutch Missionary Society turned over a predominantly Chinese congregation in Kayuapu to the Mennonite Mission in recognition of comity agreements in which Kayuapu fell within the Mennonite zone. Periodically, the Mission renewed its efforts to reach out to the Chinese community. In 1910, for example, Johann Fast, a Mennonite missionary from Russia, hired Nicolas Loupolly as an evangelist to the Chinese because he spoke Malay; in 1913, after that effort failed, Fast hired Yap Boen Pho, who preached in Chinese.

But despite these efforts, the focus of the Mennonite Mission remained primarily on rural Javanese and the model of self-sufficient agricultural communities, far from the cities where Chinese immigrants tended to settle. Seventy years after the arrival of the first Dutch Mennonite missionaries, only a few members of the Chinese community in the Muria region had been integrated into the congregations associated with the Mission, and most of those individuals had already been Christians when they emigrated from China.

THE BEGINNINGS OF KUDUS MOVEMENT: TEE SIEM TAT AND SIE DJOEN NIO

The emergence of a church in the Chinese community with strong connections to the Mennonite tradition was largely thanks to the efforts of a remarkable individual from the Central Javanese town of Kudus—Tee Siem Tat (1872–1940)—along with his wife, Sie Djoen Nio (1875–1962). In the early 1920s, Tee Siem Tat was active in a number of successful businesses. His largest enterprise was printing wrappers for the clove cigarette industry that was booming in Kudus, but he also had controlling interest in several other factories.

Though nominally Confucian, the couple had been exposed to Christianity. Their three children, for example, attended a Catholic mission school in Kudus, and in 1908 they allowed their children to be baptized into the Catholic Church. Around the same time, a relative of Sie Djoen Nio gave her a Bible, translated into Malay by Mennonite missionary H. C. Klinkert, which she began to read with great interest. Sie Djoen Nio was deeply moved by the stories in the Gospels, particularly the account of Christ's suffering and sacrifice. Initially, Tee Siem Tat was troubled by his wife's newfound religious devotion, worried that the Chinese community would react negatively if they were to adopt the "Dutch religion." But in 1917, he became

Wife and husband Sie Djoen Nio (left) and Tee Siem Tat (right), founders of GKMI. PHOTOGRAPH COURTESY OF GKMI

sick. He turned first to the local shaman, and then to the priest at the Chinese temple. When that failed to bring him relief, he consulted a Western medical doctor, again to no avail.

Recalling the biblical stories of healing performed by Jesus and his disciples, Sie Djoen Nio eventually convinced her husband to seek help from a Christian pastor. Through Tee Siem Tat's uncle, the couple met with a general in the local Salvation Army who prayed for him and provided basic instruction in Christian teachings. Tee Siem Tat attributed the healing that followed to a miracle granted him by the God of his new faith. Soon thereafter, Tee Siem Tat himself was instrumental in the miraculous healing, following prayer, of a serious eye disease in the young daughter of a friend.

Tee Siem Tat spoke widely and enthusiastically about his experience, and soon persuaded others in the Chinese community in Kudus to explore Christianity as well. Eager to find a church home, he was disappointed to learn that the Salvation Army refused to practice baptism.[86] As the circle of seekers con-

---

86. He also was bothered by the ritual attention that the Salvation Army gave to the flag in the church.

tinued to grow, Tee Siem Tat then reached out to a Seventh-day Adventist group. Here too, however, he was troubled by doctrinal issues, including the Adventist prohibition against eating pork, which for many Chinese was an important part of their diet. Tee Siem Tat turned next to an independent mission in Salatiga, but they turned him away because the mission's comity agreement with the government did not include Kudus. He also disagreed with the church's practice of infant baptism, since he could not find it practiced in Scripture. It was the representatives of the Salatiga Mission who pointed Tee Siem Tat in the direction of the Mennonites.

When Tee Siem Tat approached the Mennonite Mission, the missionaries' initial reaction was very positive—for the first time, it seemed, they had a solid point of entry into the Chinese community. Tee Siem Tat also strongly affirmed Mennonite teachings on adult baptism, their emphasis on practical discipleship, and their view of the church as a visible community, separate from the government. On December 6, 1920, Nicolai Thiessen and Johann Huebert baptized Tee Siem Tat and Sie Djoen Nio in the couple's home, along with twenty-three others who had joined Tee Siem Tat's group. The new believers met in three locations in Kudus, with the Mennonite Mission supporting the new church with catechism classes and sermons and by officiating at baptisms. Over the next three years, the group celebrated sixty-three additional baptisms; by 1926, it had grown to 107 members.

Historian Lawrence Yoder has identified several reasons behind the rapid growth of the Kudus congregation.[87] Clearly, Tee Siem Tat played a crucial role. As a respected businessman

---

87. Yoder, *Muria Story*, 58–61.

and dynamic personality, he was a trusted and influential figure in the Chinese community who could communicate easily
in Malay. It also helped that new converts tended to join the
church as families. "Bring the head of the family to Christ,"
Tee Siem Tat claimed, "and other members of the family will
be won for Christ as well."[88] Furthermore, the ministry was
accompanied by "signs and wonders"—as many new converts
testified to miraculous healings or deliverance from other forms
of bondage. And lay members spoke freely and enthusiastically
about their experiences to others. Soon, additional congregations emerged in Pati and Juana, largely as the result of Tee
Siem Tat's enthusiastic witness.

The immediate—and enduring—challenge for the new
group was one of internal structure and polity, and the ongoing role that the Mission would play in shaping the identity
of the emerging church. This question came into focus almost
immediately when, two months after his baptism, Tee Siem
Tat requested that the Mission ordain him so he could officiate at baptism services and preside at communion. His request
met with immediate resistance. In the early 1920s not a single Javanese gospel teacher had been ordained by the Mission.
Instead, the Mission assured him that they would supply ministers every three months to oversee baptisms and communion
in the growing congregations.

Frustrated, and fearing that the Mission remained focused
primarily on the Javanese congregations, Tee Siem Tat simply
moved forward on his own initiative. As noted earlier, in 1925,
the Kudus congregation formally organized itself with a constitution and a plan for financial self-sufficiency. Tee's son-in-law,

---

88. Stefanus Christian Haryono, "Mennonite History and Identity in Indonesia,"
Mission Focus: Annual Review 9 (2001): 65.

Tan King Ien, was chair of the congregation; Tee Siem Tat would be the group's pastor. In early 1927, the government formally recognized the congregation, the Chinese Mennonite Christian Church.

All of these actions had been undertaken independent from the Mission. In June 1927 Tee Siem Tat wrote several letters to the Conference of Missionaries, seeking its blessing for the group's independence. The Mission did not respond. Then, on August 21, the Governor General of Netherlands Indies granted a request that the Kudus congregation be licensed for evangelistic work and that two elders, Tee Siem Tat and Oei Tjien Gie, be recognized as ministers of their church, thereby bypassing the need for ordination by the Mission. Almost immediately, the congregation began raising funds for a church building in Kudus, with construction beginning in February of 1928.[89] Again, these initiatives seem to have taken the missionaries by surprise.

When the full extent of Tee Siem Tat's actions became clear, the elderly missionary Johann Fast retired, frustrated that his efforts to work among the Chinese had been made irrelevant by the Kudus congregation. Tensions between the Kudus congregation and the Mission increased. On the one hand, recognizing that the Kudus congregation now held a license to evangelize among the Chinese in the Semarang region, in 1930 the Mission decided to turn over its largely Chinese congregations in Pati, Juana, Tayu, and Jepara to Tee Siem Tat. At the same time, however, it withdrew financial support for those congregations, even as it moved forward with its plans to replace Fast with a young German missionary, Hermann Schmitt, as

---

89. The church was rebuilt in 1941 and again in 1997.

its representative in Kudus. The Mission claimed that Schmitt would work only with Javanese in the city, but Tee Siem Tat's congregation had a significant number of Javanese members at the time, and he resisted a view of the church that was defined by ethnic identity. In that spirit, he asked the Mennonite Mission to recognize the Kudus church as its mission partner for the outreach in the Semarang region around the city, working according to geographical rather than ethnic categories. Schmitt, he argued, should stay in Kayuapu or Pati. Why should the Mission have money to support Schmitt's work in Kudus, he asked, but not acknowledge his own work in the city?

Finally, on August 22, 1930, Tee Siem Tat sent a letter to the Conference of Missionaries announcing that the Kudus congregation was breaking its ties with the Mennonite (Doopsgezinde) identity. Since they were not receiving financial support, they would no longer send reports to Schmitt or the Conference. Tee Siem Tat closed his letter "with many greetings." "We're still brethren in the Lord Jesus," he wrote, "only the brand is different."[90]

In the years that followed, Tee Siem Tat, Sie Djoen Nio, and other evangelists from the Kudus congregation traveled through the region, freely sharing their faith. In Pati, after a revival meeting in 1937 that featured John Sung of China ("the apostle of Asia"), a congregation emerged out of a Chinese house fellowship that Tee Siem Tat had formed there, which joined with another group under the informal leadership of Nelly "Mother" Tan. Nelly Tan soon became a legendary lay leader in the Pati

90. Sukoco and Yoder, *Way of the Gospel*, 239. In fact, Tee did not actually follow through with a legal name change. Although in the 1940s the group used the Chinese name Tiong Hwa Kie Tok Kauw Hwee, it remained registered as the Chinese Mennonite Christian Church until 1958, when it officially became the Gereja Kristen Muria Indonesia (GKMI, or Muria Christian Church of Indonesia).

congregation. Not only did her house-to-house evangelism result in numerous baptized members, but at one point she also raised funds to purchase a local gambling house/brothel in Pati, which she converted into a church. Thanks to her influence, along with the significant role of Sie Djoen Nio, the emerging Chinese congregation recognized the role of women in various church offices.

In addition to the thriving congregations in Kudus and Pati, Tee Siem Tat's evangelistic efforts led to the formation of other small house gatherings in towns such as Bangsri, Welahan, Mayong, and Tanjung that eventually grew into congregations. Although their evangelistic outreach was most successful in the Chinese community, Tee Siem Tat also welcomed Ambonese, Menadonese, and Javanese members into churches he helped plant. In 1941 an existing Chinese Assembly of God congregation in Demak would join the Kudus circle, further enlarging the number of churches associated with Tee Siem Tat's leadership.

In the meantime, however, questions persisted regarding the structure of the congregations associated with the Kudus church, shaped in part by Tee Siem Tat's own significant role in the growing movement. Most of the church offices, for example, were filled with members of Tee Siem Tat's family. And most of the financing for the Kudus congregation, including a short-lived dairy operation, came from Tee Siem Tat or his businesses.[91] The small house fellowships—or branch congregations—that emerged thanks to evangelistic efforts were clearly

---

91. As Paulus Widjaja has noted, "the strong role of lay leaders and the spirit of financial independence become a legacy that can still be found among the GKMI churches today." Email to author, January 28, 2021.

understood to be extensions of the Kudus congregation, under Tee Siem Tat's leadership, and not autonomous churches.

The organizational question became more complicated in the early 1930s when Tee Siem Tat received permission from both town officials in Jepara, as well as the head of Jepara's Chinese cultural and religious organization, to host church services in the home of a Chinese Christian there. By the end of 1933, a flourishing congregation had emerged in Jepara with thirty-five baptized members; two years later, it had grown to seventy-seven members. Most of the ethnic Chinese members of the Jepara congregation, however, were recent immigrants who did not connect well with the group in Kudus. When the congregation officially incorporated in December of 1935, it initially sought government recognition by identifying itself as part of the Kudus church. In June of 1935, however, the Jepara congregation had adopted the name Chinese Christian Church, suggesting that it understood itself to be distinct from the Kudus group, rather than an extension of the Kudus congregation. Although the Jepara congregation did not include the word "Mennonite" in their name, the new church body described its mission as "forming and caring for the Chinese Mennonite Christian congregations in the Jepara-Rembang (Pati) residency." Its second stated purpose was to establish schools and hospitals in the region, and its articles of incorporation envisioned a board that would have authority over the congregations in its oversight, including control over the ordination of pastors. As a further declaration of independence from the Kudus group, members of the congregational board needed to be men "from Jepara."[92]

---

92. Yoder, *Muria Story*, 97–101.

In 1936, Gombak Sugeng, a cousin of Sie Djoen Nio, was ordained as the minister of the Jepara congregation. Gombak Sugeng had been a highly respected leader in the Chinese religious and cultural community of Jepara. He spoke Dutch, and was a gifted teacher and healer. He himself had been cured of an addiction to gambling, and his ministry often included miracles of physical and emotional healing.[93] Gombak Sugeng also had a reputation for drawing a sharp line with traditional Chinese religious practices, and created alternative rituals for weddings, funerals, and other occasions celebrated within the congregation.

Uncertainties about the organizational structure and future leadership of the eight growing Chinese congregations in the Muria region were exacerbated by the sudden death of Tee Siem Tat on October 2, 1940. In the fall of 1941, Pouw Peng Hong, the pastor of the Kudus congregation, proposed a meeting of all the Chinese Christian churches in the region to discuss the creation of a "Muria Area Church Order." In the document that emerged from the gathering, most of the detail focused on the spiritual life of the local congregations, with a strong emphasis on repentance, followed by baptism on confession of faith, and a life of holiness. Healing and evangelism were expressions of a holy life. Church councils were to be selected by majority vote and served for life.

What the Church Order did not clarify, however, was whether Kudus was understood to be the mother church that presided over the congregations, including Jepara, or if the emerging model was to be a true synod, with all congregations relating on an equal status. Also left unresolved was the question of how the church was to function in the absence of Tee

---

93. Gombak Sugeng reportedly cut off his own right thumb, so that he would no longer be able to hold playing cards in his hand.

Siem Tat, especially since his family businesses supported much of the church's work, and because his son-in-law Tan King Ien continued to hold a great deal of informal authority. At the same time, relations with the Dutch Mission remained problematic, especially since the Conference of Missionaries, much to the irritation of the Kudus leaders, continued to include data from the Kudus group in their reports as if it was playing an important role in the life of the Chinese congregations.

NAVIGATING TRAUMA AND DECLINE

Even as these questions were unfolding, global events were creating a crisis of a different sort. As also recounted earlier, in the spring of 1940, Germany invaded and occupied the Netherlands, which immediately raised questions about Indonesia's status as a Dutch colony. Then, after the attack on Pearl Harbor in December 1941, Japan occupied much of Southeast Asia, including Indonesia. Presenting themselves as liberators, the Japanese occupiers aligned themselves with the Muslim community over against those groups who were associated with Dutch rule—namely, Christians and ethnic Chinese.

In March 1942, shortly after the Japanese landed on the coast of north Central Java, Muslim youth began attacking Chinese communities, looting stores, destroying homes, raping women, and circumcising Chinese men. The attack soon broadened to include Javanese Christians, resulting in the destruction of church buildings in Tegalombo and Margorejo, an attack on the leprosarium in Donorojo, and violence directed toward the hospital in Tayu that led to the death of a missionary and several local attendants. The Muslim youth movement, known as Ansor, then turned to the larger towns of Pati and Kudus. Surprisingly, the Chinese church in Pati was saved when an Ansor leader reportedly announced, "This is the house of the Lord Jesus," and passed on.

When Japanese authorities began their own attacks, church leaders in Jepara and Kudus successfully persuaded them that their congregations had no connection with the Dutch or with the Mennonite Mission. The Japanese contented themselves with banning the use of the Chinese language, shuttering church-related schools, and demanding that the Salvation Army hymnal used by the Kudus congregations—which depicted the congregation as an army—be replaced, which had the salutary effect of leading church members to create their own songbook. In general, Chinese Christians in the cities of the Muria region experienced less persecution than the Javanese churches during the occupation.

In the years immediately after the end of World War II, the Muria Chinese congregations showed genuine signs of vibrancy. Membership in the churches in Kudus, Pati, and Jepara, for example, grew significantly in the early 1940s. For the first time, the Kudus congregation ordained a Javanese pastor—Sudarsohadi Notodihardjo—who would also eventually serve as chair of the synod. And several congregations began sending gifted young people to seminaries for theological training.

But the postwar years raised familiar questions for the church regarding polity, and several new questions about theology. In April 1948, representatives of the eight congregations met to again clarify their organizational structure. Building on the draft of the 1941 Church Order, the new document—which marked the official creation of the Muria Christian Church—described the group as "an association of Chinese Christian churches that is made up of members of Chinese Christian congregations in Kudus, Jepara, Mayong, Pati, Bangsri, Welahan,

Demak, Tanjung, and other congregations not named here." The document sought to balance the authority of individual congregations against the claims of the Kudus congregation as the "mother church" and the descendants of Tee Siem Tat who, in line with traditional Chinese culture, also exercised a kind of paternal authority within the church.

The new structure envisioned congregations run by councils whose members served for two-year renewable terms. The synod claimed the authority to review ministers and to make official appointments, but ministers were called and ordained by the congregations. The synod's tasks were focused on overseeing the liturgy used in worship, along with evangelism, literature distribution, pulpit exchanges, catechism materials, and membership statistics.[94] Its finances were to be supported by contributions from congregations, which varied according to their capacity.

Chairing the synod, beginning in April 1948, was Tan King Ien, Tee Siem Tat's son-in-law, and it was assumed that the Kudus congregation would continue to play a significant role in the organization. But the new Church Order gave little attention to the logistics of how the work of the synod would actually be structured, how often it would meet, and how far its authority extended over the individual congregations.

At the same time, Mennonite Central Committee—which, at the request of the Mennonite Church in the Netherlands, was just beginning its work in Indonesia—introduced a new, complicated dynamic into the life of the Chinese congregations. MCC correctly perceived a need for more intentional theological training, and offered to send two ministerial candidates in the Muria Christian Church to the United States for

---

94. In 1952, the synod reported 541 baptized members in seven congregations. Yoder, *Muria Story*, 155.

seminary education if the synod would share in the finances. Tan King Ien, who had inherited a successful printing business from Tee Siem Tat and continued to exercise significant influence within the Kudus congregation, was quick to respond. His son, Tan Hao An (1922–2003)—better known by his English name Herman Tan—had expressed interest in studying at the Jakarta Theological Seminary or at the Mennonite seminary in Amsterdam. In December 1949, Tan King Ien informed MCC executive secretary Orie O. Miller, who was visiting Kudus, that since the synod had few financial resources, he would personally fund the church's portion of Herman's education.

So Herman Tan traveled to the United States and began studying at the Mennonite Biblical Seminary in Goshen, Indiana, under the tutelage of Harold S. Bender. Tan King Ien regarded the arrangement as a personal opportunity; MCC understood its support as a collaboration with the Kudus synod. When Herman and his wife, Jo, returned to Java late in 1954, eager to implement ideas shaped by their theological studies in Mennonite institutions, they faced a somewhat hostile reception from other church leaders.

Similar tensions had emerged in 1952, when Mennonite World Conference invited a representative from the Muria Christian Church to attend its global assembly in Basel. Again, MCC agreed to pay half the costs. But when the synod balked at paying the other half, Tan King Ien covered the costs out of his own funds, and departed in July 1952 just before the annual meeting of the synod. Accompanying him was Soehadiweko Djojodihardjo, chair of Javanese Mennonite Church synod.

Tan King Ien was gone for five months. In his absence, the synod—frustrated by the ongoing dominance of Tee Siem Tat's family—passed a series of decisions that weakened his authority as chair. The Kudus church council also removed him as congregational chair, and then took the further step of removing him as its minister. When he returned, Tan King Ien found himself virtually exiled from the congregation.[95]

In the 1950s, the Muria synod, which had grown rapidly in the years immediately after the war, slowly declined in membership and faced growing financial difficulties. Tan King Ien continued to serve as the synod's chair until the seventh general synod assembly, held in Jepara in 1956. After Tan King Ien's resignation, the synod proceeded to elect his son, Herman Tan, as its new leader. In the years that followed, Herman and others walked a delicate balance in maintaining relations with the Kudus congregation while also attempting to strengthen the identity and authority of the synod.

When, for example, Liem Liong Tjoen, who had been hired in 1951 as the first paid, full-time minister, attempted to introduce a new liturgy in the Kudus congregation that aligned more closely with the Reformed Church, Herman and Jo Tan led an opposition group, which was eager to anchor the congregation and the synod more explicitly in Anabaptist-Mennonite principles. Liem Liong Tjoen's proposal that the Muria Chinese congregations merge with the large Chinese Presbyterian synod of Central Java also created tension, leading finally to his resignation from the Kudus congregation in 1959 and Tan King Ien's restoration as pastor.

Another expression of the synod's struggle to clarify its identity were ongoing debates about theology, especially regarding differences that emerged between supporters of the revolutionary Indonesian nationalist movement and those shaped by postwar

---

95. Yoder, *Muria Story*, 165–67.

encounters with Mennonites from North America. In the tradition of Tee Siem Tat, formal theology had never been a central
concern among the Muria Chinese congregations. The focus of
evangelism was on repentance, salvation, baptism, and blessing, in the expectation of eternal life with God. Moreover, the
Muria Chinese churches had never claimed pacifism as a central
part of their theological identity. Indeed, in the context of the
Indonesian War of Independence, many young people in the
church eagerly joined the Chinese Christian Youth Movement
as an expression of patriotic loyalty to the new Indonesian state.

So Herman Tan was introducing something new in 1958
when he proposed that the synod adopt a twenty-point confession of faith, along with a new liturgy, that drew heavily
on insights and examples he encountered among Mennonite
churches in North America. The faith statement—which
Herman claimed had been personally approved by Harold S.
Bender—included standard affirmations of orthodox Christian
belief as well as several distinctive Anabaptist-Mennonite principles such as adult baptism, the centrality of discipleship, and
a rejection of the oath. The confession included a general statement on peace, though it avoided taking a firm position against
participation in the military. The synod ultimately adopted the
liturgy and confession of faith that Herman Tan put forward,
though not all the congregations were equally enthused.

The same 1958 synod meeting also took up the question of
the group's name. The Kudus congregation wanted the churches in the synod to adopt the name "Christian Church of [name
of the city]," whereas the Jepara congregation advocated for
the name "Indonesian Christian Church." After much debate,
Herman Tan sought to resolve the tension by registering the
synod with the notary public under the official name Synod of

the Muria Christian Churches of Indonesia (Persatuan Gereja-Gereja Kristen Muria Indonesia–PGKMI).

NEW GENERATIONS

Though they faced opposition from an older generation of leaders, Herman Tan and others in a younger generation of emerging leaders—including Charles Christano, Albert Widjaja, Mesach Krisetya, Andreas Setiawan, Adi Sutjipta, Chrismanto Jonathan, Adi Sutanto, and others—would go on to play very significant roles in the life of the GKMI church during the last decades of the twentieth century. These young people, many of them among the first to attend seminary or pursue theological studies, brought a new vision for channeling the evangelistic mission of the church into institutional forms beyond the congregations in ways that an older generation of leaders, who were used to guarding congregational autonomy, often found threatening. Complicating matters, the energy of these young people found ready allies and financial support from postwar European and North American Mennonite relief and mission organizations who were quite accustomed to thinking of the work of the church in institutional forms.

One expression of this new, potentially threatening, form of organization were the Bible camps that Herman Tan, along with Charles Christano, Albert Widjaja, Mesach Krisetya, and others, helped to organize. Beginning in 1956, as many as two hundred to three hundred GKMI youth gathered annually for a week of revival meetings, Bible studies, and lectures that also served as a training ground for exercising leadership gifts. Jo Tan was instrumental in forming various women's organizations, which helped expand the number of women who served on local church councils.

In 1965, Herman Tan and others formed the Foundation for Missions and Charities (PIPKA) to support church planters, particularly in urban areas where GKMI youth were migrating for employment or educational opportunities. Some congregations had already been pursuing this strategy. In 1958, for example, the Jepara congregation established a branch congregation in the large city of Semarang, which soon became an independent church and a dynamic center of renewed mission activity. GKMI Semarang, in turn, would go on to establish numerous other congregations. But PIPKA brought a new level of coordination, vision, energy, and resources to the church planting and also had a vision for church growth beyond the ethnic Chinese community. With its support, new congregations emerged in cities like Surakarta, Jakarta, Kalibaru, Depok, and Cipayung. When the Indonesian government encouraged impoverished Javanese farmers to relocate to other islands where land was more plentiful, the mission extended its reach into South Sumatra and Kalimantan, and then to the islands of Celebes, Batam, and Bali.[96]

Unfortunately, PIPKA's work became the focus of ongoing contention in its early years, especially since Herman Tan, who had significant influence over how North American funds were spent, seemed to be directing resources that had once supported the synod into PIPKA, which operated outside the formal control of the synod.[97] Eventually, however, PIPKA was turned

---

96. A significant number of poor farmers from the GITJ synod also transmigrated to these areas, leading to strong GITJ congregations in the provinces of Lampung and South Sumatra.

97. Late in 1965, Tan and his family moved to Jakarta, where he intended to plant a church and start a Christian radio program. With Tan now far from the Muria region, the synod acted to remove him as its chair. Four years later, Tan relocated to the United States, where he spent the remainder of his life.

over to the synod, where it has since become the GKMI's main mission organization. By 2010, PIPKA was supporting eighty-two mission posts, drawing on support from GKMI congregations as well as various Western mission agencies.[98] PIPKA also reported that seventeen of its former mission posts had become full-fledged GKMI congregations.

This new organizational energy spilled over into publishing ventures, with the formation of Muria Churches Publishers—whose books focused initially on Sunday school curriculum and texts related to Anabaptist-Mennonite history and theology. In 1967, the synod began to publish a regular periodical, *Berita GKMI*, to keep congregations informed about the church's broader activities.

GKMI was also pulled into the larger Anabaptist-Mennonite community through a host of new international relationships. In 1962, for example, GKMI applied for membership in Mennonite World Conference, where leaders from the postwar generation—people like Charles Christano, Mesach Krisetya, and Albert Widjaja—would eventually assume significant responsibilities.[99] Shortly thereafter, it became an active member in the Asia Mennonite Conference. Beginning in 1969, young people from GKMI began to participate in the International Visitor Exchange Program (IVEP), sponsored by MCC. Within a decade more than fifty young GKMI members had spent a year doing volunteer work in North America, bringing back

98. Included in the partnership agreement was a commitment that Mennonite missionaries from Europe and North America would not plant churches in Indonesia that were identified by their own denominational name (e.g., General Conference, Mennonite Brethren). All new churches were to be part of the Muria Christian Church of Indonesia.

99. Albert Widjaja would go on to also become actively involved in the leadership of both the National Council (now Communion) of Churches in Indonesia (PGI) and the Christian Conference of Asia (CCA).

new insights, skills, and perspectives to share with the church in Java. The traumatic impact of the mob attacks on the Chinese community in 1965 also had the effect of opening up the synod to new partnerships, including a collaboration with GITJ in support of the Wiyata Wacana theological school in Pati that received funding from both European and North American Mennonites.

In addition to the outreach of the GKMI synod and various parachurch initiatives like the Ichtus radio station in Semarang, several congregations—particularly those in Kudus and Jepara—also pursued their own social ministries. The Kudus congregation, for example, actively supported a clinic under the Kudus Christian Health Foundation, and both Jepara and Kudus were strong advocates for church-related primary and secondary education.

Interior of the GKMI Kudus church. The striking stained glass windows were designed by Charles Cristano, long-time GKMI pastor, synod leader, and president of Mennonite World Conference from 1978 to 1984.
PHOTOGRAPH COURTESY OF DANIEL TALENTA

During the last decades of the twentieth century, the GKMI consolidated many of its programs and international relationships. PIPKA—with assistance from Eastern Mennonite Missions and the Dutch Mennonite Mission, and through collaborations with Mennonite churches in Hong Kong and the Philippines—has flourished, broadening the identity of the GKMI church to include ethnic groups throughout the Indonesian archipelago, even sending missionaries to Singapore and Mongolia.[100] Today, GKMI is one of the few explicitly interethnic churches in all of Indonesia, a status which has demanded of its members a great deal of ongoing cross-cultural awareness and sensitivity.

In recent decades, GKMI synod leaders—Eddy Sutjipto (tenure 1999–2004), Aristarchus Sukarto (2004–2009), Paulus Widjaja (2009–2019), and Agus Mayanto (2019–present)— have overseen the synod's ongoing growth, with the addition of nineteen congregations between 2000 and 2017. Today, the GKMI has sixty-four churches, sixty-five branch churches, and 104 PIPKA outpost churches, spread across thirteen provinces. According to a recent thoughtful analysis by Andi Santoso of the strengths and challenges facing the GKMI, this rapid growth of the synod in geographically scattered regions of Indonesia—combined with an influx of pastors from other theological traditions—has resulted in a growing theological diversity within the GKMI synod, alongside the ethnic and cultural diversity resulting from its mission outreach.[101]

---

100. One GKMI congregation in Jakarta has members from fourteen different ethnicities. Andi Santoso, interview by author, January 2, 2021.

101. Andi Santoso, "Tantangan dan Peluang Pengejawantahan Visi Misi Sinode GKMI Periode 2009–2019" [Challenges and Opportunities of an Embodied Vision and Mission in the GKMI Synod, 2009–2019] (Semarang, 2017).

At the same time, the synod has a well-deserved reputation for valuing the gifts of laypeople and drawing on the energy of its youth. It has also worked consciously to cultivate a deeper sense of shared theological identity formation through a series of continuing education programs for pastors. The Mennonite Diakonia Service has become widely recognized for its skills in disaster management and commitment to initiatives focused on peacemaking, conflict mediation, and reconciliation. And the GKMI synod has committed itself to openly address the racial and ethnic tensions that have been a painful reality in Indonesian society.

Congregations that make up the GKMI today have a long and rich history of entrepreneurial independence, tempered by a recognition that the synod structure has provided them with crucial resources necessary for thriving evangelistic, service, and educational programs, and for a collective witness as a minority church in a pluralistic religious context.

6

The Indonesian Christian Congregation

(Jemaat Kristen Indonesia—JKI)

FROM THE EXTERIOR it seems as if one might be entering a sports arena. Located in the bustling Central Javanese city of Semarang, the Holy Stadium—home to the JKI Gospel of the Kingdom church (JKI Injil Kerajaan)—is a grand structure with multiple entrances that can easily absorb the eight thousand to twelve thousand people who worship here every Sunday morning. The Gospel of the Kingdom congregation is not the largest of the JKI network of churches. That honor goes to the JKI Jakarta Praise Community Church, which claims eighteen thousand members. But the Semarang church, which will serve as the venue for the 17th Mennonite World Conference general assembly in the summer of 2022, offers a vivid portrait into the character of the Indonesian Christian Congregation (Jemaat Kristen Indonesia, or JKI), the youngest

The Holy Stadium in Semarang, home of the JKI Gospel of the Kingdom church (JKI Injil Kerajaan) and site of the Mennonite World Conference global assembly in July 2022. PHOTOGRAPH COURTESY OF MENNONITE WORLD CONFERENCE

of the three Indonesian synods that are members of Mennonite World Conference.

Like many of the congregations in the JKI network, Gospel of the Kingdom began first as a prayer fellowship under the guidance of Hanna Sebadja, then quickly expanded to a Sunday morning charismatic worship service that attracted hundreds of participants. Under the leadership of Petrus Agung Purnomo and his wife, Tina, the group continued to expand in the late 1990s as more and more people were attracted to its unique blend of charismatic worship, energetic music, numerous social outreach programs, and the gracious relationships that the congregation cultivated with its Muslim neighbors. Today, the

Holy Stadium is a thriving community center, offering legal aid services for the poor, counseling for drug addiction, a bookstore, a thriving youth sports program, a food kitchen, and a school serving four thousand elementary and high school students. Although its programs and ministries all operate independently of the synod, Gospel of the Kingdom is one of more than three hundred congregations that make up the JKI today. Each JKI member church has its own story, of course, but the Holy Stadium captures well the JKI flavor—dynamic, colorful, confident, charismatic, theologically eclectic, culturally contextual, socially engaged, growth-oriented, and prosperous. In the JKI synod, God is a God of abundance who wants his people to flourish materially as well as spiritually.

ORIGINS OF THE JKI: A GKMI YOUTH REVIVAL

Although the JKI synod officially started in 1985, its roots reach back to the mid-1960s when a charismatic revival movement, born in the island of Timor, swept across Indonesia at precisely the moment when the Chinese community was facing one of the worst outbreaks of ethnic violence in the country's history and the GKMI church was struggling to integrate a new generation of young people into its leadership. Several promising GKMI young adults who had studied abroad were finding it difficult to share their gifts within the traditional culture of church leadership. Those who had moved to larger cities in Java for employment or educational opportunities were increasingly frustrated with the traditions and organizational structures of GKMI.

Late in 1965, Agus Suwantoro, a young member of the GKMI Bangsri congregation who had relocated to Semarang for work, took the initiative to organize other GKMI young people from his hometown into an informal fellowship.[102] The group, which they called Keluarga Sangkakala, gathered weekly for prayer and fellowship, and even published a monthly newsletter. In 1967, as Keluarga Sangkakala grew to thirty people, its planning committee—now led by twenty-year-old Agus Suwantoro—organized a youth conference at Bangsri for "Workers in the Field of the Lord" (Konferensi Pelayan Ladang Tuhan, or KPLT). Building on the assumption that every Christian was called to some form of mission, the young people viewed the gathering as an opportunity for training and inspiration.

GKMI leaders were divided in their response. Some, especially the local ministers at Bangsri, were clearly threatened by the initiative, which seemed to be moving forward outside of normal church channels. Others were skeptical that the youth would have the resources or organizational skills to carry through with the plan. But still others, including Mesach Krisetya and Charles Christano—GKMI pastors who would later become active in Mennonite World Conference—supported the initiative and agreed to participate as speakers.

In the course of the five-day conference, attended by some 225 young people, the presence of the Holy Spirit became real in several dramatic ways. The organizers had no financial backing, yet money and food miraculously appeared just when it was needed. Many who attended the gathering experienced the

---

102. Much of the detail that follows draws on Adi Sutanto, "A Strategy for Planting Churches in Java Through the Sangkakala Mission with Special Emphasis on the Javanese and Chinese People (DMiss, Fuller Theological Seminary, School of World Mission, 1986). I have also benefited greatly from the insights of Rony Chandra Kristanto, along with his "Evangelism as Public Theology: The Public Engagement of the Gospel of the Kingdom Church in Semarang, Indonesia" (PhD diss., University of Birmingham, 2018). Lydia Adi Sidharta and Adi Sutanto also read and commented on this chapter.

Spirit in the form of visions, prophecies, speaking in tongues, healing, and deliverance from evil spirits. In several instances, participants reportedly received visions that enabled them to identify and destroy fetishes—objects thought to possess spiritual power—hidden in the homes of GKMI members.

The spiritual revival initiated at the Bangsri conference soon spread to other areas, including Yogyakarta, Bandung, Jakarta, Jepara, and Kudus, nearly always led by young people. Some GKMI leaders spoke out against the charismatic elements of the youth fellowship movement, but elsewhere—in Semarang and Salatiga, for example—GKMI church leaders responded positively and participated in the formation of several new congregations that emerged from the revival.

In 1970, the young leaders of the "Old Sangkakala" movement tried to unite with PIPKA, an emerging mission program associated with GKMI. But the synod rejected the proposal and the general fervor of the revival movement began to wane. In the end, the Sangkakala initiative merged with a music group called All For Christ to become the Yayasan Christopherus, an independent, interdenominational evangelistic and service ministry.

Yet even as the original Sangkakala movement was fading from view, several early participants longed to recover the energy and fervor of the 1967 revival. In particular, Adi Sutanto, a gifted young student from Bangsri who had served as secretary of the youth fellowship group in Semarang, hungered for a deeper understanding of the renewal he had witnessed and the dynamics of church growth. From 1973 to 1976, he pursued additional education in the United States, including studies at Eastern Mennonite Seminary, Mennonite Brethren Biblical Seminary, and Fuller Theological Seminary. In June of

1976, Adi Sutanto returned to Indonesia with master's degrees in divinity and theology, eager to serve the GKMI church in the area of church growth. He was particularly interested in how the spontaneity and power of the Spirit, which he had experienced in the early Sangkakala movement, could be joined with strategic planning, organizational skills, and the best missiological insights to bring about growth and renewal in the GKMI church.

It soon became clear, however, that the scope of Adi Sutanto's vision and the insights that he had gleaned from his seminary studies did not align well with the direction of the GKMI and its mission agency. In May 1977, Adi Sutanto and several others founded a new organization called Yayasan Keluarga Sangkakala (Trumpet Family Foundation) that they hoped could carry forward something of the evangelistic, Spirit-driven character of the earlier Sangkakala movement.

The early years were challenging. Adi Sutanto taught English classes during the day, while his wife, Sri Padmawati Adi, pursued a law degree at the University of Diponegoro. In the evenings he preached and led prayer groups in the couple's home in Semarang. Those prayer meetings soon multiplied. By the end of 1979, seven house fellowships of twenty to sixty people were meeting regularly in Semarang; six months later, they had increased to fourteen groups. In September of 1980, a group of around three hundred who called themselves "Charismatic Worship Service" (Kebaktian Kharismatik) began to meet in a rented city hall. By 1984, the revived Sangkakala movement in Semarang numbered sixteen hundred people, meeting in forty-six different groups.

Participants in the house fellowships encountered church there in a dramatically new way. The small groups offered an authentic religious experience, in the supportive context of a family home, that spoke directly to their physical, emotional, financial, and spiritual needs. The weekly evening services usually consisted of prayer, singing, Bible study, preaching, testimonies, and offerings, followed by refreshments. In contrast to the established churches, the house fellowships called on all participants to exercise their gifts. Each month, the groups celebrated the Lord's Supper, and Adi Sutanto organized catechism classes for new believers before their baptism.

Parallel to the growth of the Yayasan Keluarga Sangkakala prayer groups in Semarang, other aspects of the ministry were rapidly developing as well. In July 1977, Adi Sutanto began to publish a monthly newsletter, *Gema Sangkakala*. The periodical gradually evolved into a magazine, which proved crucial to the financial success of the ministry. The funds that flowed in after each new issue soon enabled him to devote all his energies to the growing ministry. In 1978 a Semarang house fellowship member also started a cassette tape ministry, freely distributing recordings of sermons from the revival meetings as a form of evangelism. Other participants organized a musical group that quickly became an integral part of the campaigns. By the following spring, the Sangkakala ministry was able to open an office.

At the same time, the movement was also expanding elsewhere through a series of revival campaigns. Already in July 1977, Adi Sutanto began holding open air evangelistic meetings, first in the village of Ngaglik, then Bondo and Sampetan, and then in Semarang. The fruits of the revival campaigns were soon apparent. By the following year, Yayasan Keluarga Sangkakala was holding ten to fifteen campaigns a year, many of them focused especially on young people, that resulted in thousands of commitments. Adi Sutanto generally preached, but he also frequently invited other evangelists or emerging lay leaders within the movement to share in that task. Most of the meetings included lively music, healing services, speaking in tongues, and burning of fetishes.

The Yayasan Keluarga Sangkakala revival meetings that started in Javanese cities like Kudus, Pati, Tayu, Jepara, Salatiga, Magelang, and Yogyakarta broadened to include other Indonesian islands such as Bali, Sumba, Timor, and Sulawesi. By 1981, Sangkakala revival campaigns extended to Malaysia, Singapore, the Philippines, and South Korea. In many places, though not all, the gatherings resulted in the formation of new congregations that continued to relate to the Sangkakala organization.

When registering with the Central Javanese Department of Religion in 1979, the Yayasan Keluarga Sangkakala identified its primary purpose as evangelism. But when its charter was confirmed with the central government of Indonesia four years later, its mission had expanded to include authorization to build churches, hospitals, clinics, and schools. Over time, this growing concern for social ministries was to become a prominent feature of the Sangkakala movement.

FROM YAYASAN KELUARGA SANGKAKALA TO JKI (INDONESIAN CHRISTIAN CONGREGATION)

Throughout the early years of Sangkakala's expansion, Adi Sutanto had remained a member of the GKMI church. Initially, he was clear that he did not intend to plant churches or to start a new denomination. Yayasan Keluarga Sangkakala was a parachurch organization focused on evangelism and revival in which he served as executive director and reported to a board. But it was not a church. Indeed, as soon as any congregation that emerged from the evangelistic work of Sangkakala gained legal recognition, it was considered to be an independent body. That posture changed, however, when Adi Sutanto recognized that many of those who experienced conversion in the revival meetings either were not finding their way into existing churches after the campaign moved on or were in communities without any local church options.[103]

In 1985, the Sangkakala movement began to baptize new converts into a fellowship called Jemaat Kristen Indonesia Hosana. The first church plant was JKI Imanuel, in the village of Sampetan. Around the same time, Adi Sutanto also started an outreach to Indonesian students and immigrants in Los Angeles and, in 1983, invited Herman Tan—who was then living in Indiana—to serve as a pastor to the emerging congregation.

The evolving structure of the movement was also shaped by developments in GKMI. In the early 1980s the success of Yayasan Keluarga Sangkakala helped revive memories among some GKMI members of the 1967 Bangsri Sangkakala movement and sparked a renewed interest in more charismatic forms of worship within the GKMI. According to some sources, Adi Sutanto, hoping to avoid a division, invited GKMI leaders to integrate the Yayasan Keluarga Sangkakala ministry into the synod's existing structure. That overture, however, collapsed when synod leaders insisted that Sangkakala distance itself from the charismatic elements of its identity.

At the same time, a new government regulation required all prayer groups that worshiped on Sunday to register as a synod or denomination. So, in 1985, Yayasan Keluarga Sangkakala

---

103. Adi Sutanto, "Strategy for Planting Churches," 33–34.

complied with the new law and formally incorporated as a new synod called Jemaat Kristen Indonesia (JKI, or Indonesian Christian Congregation).[104] Around the same time, internal tensions within the GKMI Kudus congregation related to control of a hospital foundation led to the formation of several new groups who briefly identified themselves as GKMII (Gereja Kristen Muria Indonesia Injili). In 1985, the Minister of Religion in Central Java helped to adjudicate an understanding in which one of the new groups, the more charismatic GKMII Ladang Baru, merged with the newly formed JKI. A second GKMII group returned to the GKMI.

These developments marked a significant new chapter in the unfolding story of the Yayasan Keluarga Sangkakala movement. With the formation of the JKI synod in 1985, the Sangkakala movement shifted in character from a parachurch organization to assuming some—though not all—of the features often associated with a denomination. The history of the JKI since then has been a creative balance between maintaining the charismatic dynamic central to its original DNA and providing the institutional structure and form needed to adequately support the growing network of congregations it serves.

Some of the continuities between the Yayasan Keluarga Sangkakala and the JKI were obvious. Adi Sutanto, for example, continued to play a crucial role as JKI's spiritual leader. The JKI maintained a strong focus on youth, music, and social ministries. And the new synod continued the Sangkakala focus on evangelism and church growth.

But JKI also had characteristics of a synod. In his 1986 doctoral dissertation on the Sangkakala movement, Adi Sutanto

---

104. In 1989 the JKI received registered legal status with the Indonesian Ministry of Religion.

identified several qualities he hoped would distinguish JKI from the GITJ and GKMI synods. In the JKI context, the charismatic gifts of the Holy Spirit were not simply an integral part of the individual Christian experience; they were a crucial dimension of church growth that spoke directly to the Indonesian context. "In planting churches in Java among people that are animistic," Adi Sutanto wrote, "we really need the power of the Holy Spirit, because . . . it is particularly in animistic societies that the cosmic struggle between Christ and Satan is most apparent."[105] In the Indonesian context, prayer, fasting, and evidence of the power of the Holy Spirit mattered more than doctrinal confessions, debates over church polity, or denominational distinctives. The "signs and wonders" that accompany Christian witness—healings, deliverance, testing of spirits, battles with the demonic—Adi Sutanto insisted, were all "essential for effective ministry in Indonesia," where natural formations like mountains, stones, and trees were closely linked to ancestral spirits, and mystics demonstrated their power by performing miracles.

In a closely related way, Adi Sutanto was convinced that a successful church in Indonesia could not be dependent on Western sources of funding or theology. "We want to plant indigenous churches," he wrote. "The term 'indigenous' is significant because the churches in the third world countries which were planted by the western missionaries, were for many years still 'foreign.'. . . In their government, finance, and efforts to propagate the gospel they were completely controlled

---

105. Adi Sutanto, "Strategy for Planting Churches," 79. "Out of 3,779 verses in all four Gospels," Adi Sutanto noted, "727 are directly connected with both physical and mental healing. Beside this, thirty-one additional verses mention in general themes about the miracles involving healing." Adi Sutanto, 87.

by the missionaries. Only later was it realized that this is not healthy."[106]

For truly indigenous churches to develop, he continued, it must be clear from the beginning that any financial support would be gradually decreased.[107]

Adi Sutanto was also concerned that Indonesian churches take responsibility to develop their own theology. "The influence of western theology is very strong in our Indonesian churches today," he noted.

> This influence came naturally because the Gospel was brought
> by western missionaries. . . . Instead of receiving the pure
> Gospel, we received a Gospel that has been colored by western
> culture and world view. The influence of western culture
> is found in almost all aspects of our church life. From the
> curriculum of theological schools, liturgy for worship, hymns
> and spiritual songs, to even the vestments of our pastors, all
> are derived from the West. In spite of the warm tropical cli-
> mate of our country, our pastors today still wear their Dutch
> style black and thick gowns, even though we do not find this
> custom in the Bible. This is a simple but clear example.[108]

By contrast, he argued, the Sangkakala movement,

> came into being and developed with its own unique
> Indonesian identity. In other words, Sangkakala is indigenous.

---

106. Adi Sutanto, "Strategy for Planting Churches," 137.

107. "Whether the church planter is going to continue to be the pastor of the new church or not, that particular church, from her birth, must be challenged to support herself. The matter of financial support is very important because in general, the new congregation will never be independent in other areas if she is still financially dependent." Adi Sutanto, "Strategy for Planting Churches," 138.

108. Adi Sutanto, "Strategy for Planting Churches," 97.

From the start, Sangkakala was independent in its government, [financial] support, as well as in propagating the Gospel. From a cultural standpoint, Sangkakala did not incorporate anything from Western countries. This is a positive aspect because in this way Sangkakala is not considered something foreign by the people around it. . . . Even though Sangkakala may always be criticized in some ways, it has never been accused of being "America" or something "imported from other Western countries."[109]

In his view, every new church had an imperative to assume responsibility for its own ministries, including such details as how the congregation was going to arrange its seating, how the Sunday school would be organized, the form that testimonies and prayer would take within the congregation, as well as the nature of its various external ministries.[110]

Finally, Adi Sutanto's emphasis on nurturing churches that were financially independent and ecclesially mature pointed to his conviction that the local congregation was the primary expression of the Spirit's work in the world. In this sense, he came down solidly on one side of a long-standing tension within the Indonesian Anabaptist-Mennonite synods about church polity. Since the church, he argued, "is a spiritual movement . . . and takes a form that varies from culture to culture," any church structure beyond the context in which the local congregation is situated must be very flexible.[111]

---

109. Adi Sutanto, "Strategy for Planting Churches," 58.
110. Adi Sutanto, "Strategy for Planting Churches," 139.
111. Adi Sutanto, "Strategy for Planting Churches," 140. Adi Sutanto devoted two long chapters in his dissertation to the distinctive cultural characteristics of the Chinese and Javanese groups in Indonesia, drawing implications from these observations for very different strategies for church planting.

This last point—emerging in part, no doubt, from the frustration early Sangkakala leaders experienced with the administrative structures of the GKMI synod—would prove to be more complicated as the newly formed JKI synod took shape. It was not that the synod wished to exert tight control over the internal operations of its member congregations, but Adi Sutanto and his colleagues recognized that some institutional structure was essential if the JKI vision was going to endure. Already in his 1986 dissertation, for example, Adi Sutanto noted that a major weakness of his evangelization campaigns was the lack of an organized structure to support new converts with adequate biblical instruction and a church home.[112] He also clearly recognized the value of strategic planning—with careful goal setting and rational plans for achieving those goals. Even more crucial was the need for theological education to prepare lay leaders for Christian ministry.

THE JKI SYNOD TODAY

In 1986, Adi Sutanto announced a goal of planting five hundred congregations by the year 2000. That did not happen, largely because the form of congregational life that characterized the early years of the Sangkakala movement—small, decentralized house fellowships—shifted dramatically in the following years, especially in urban contexts, with the emergence of megachurches. Megachurches seemed to offer an effective strategy for providing a highly polished Sunday morning worship experience—with professional musicians, along with a host of specialized programs, and a range of social ministries—while preserving the intimacy of house fellowships in the form

---

112. Adi Sutanto, "Strategy for Planting Churches," 96.

of small groups that met for prayer and Bible study at some point during the week. In urban settings, megachurches appealed particularly to upwardly mobile young professionals who expected their church to have the same standards of polish and excellence as their work environment.

In addition to planting churches of its own, JKI soon became known as a synod that provided a diverse group of existing congregations—from house churches to megachurches—with spiritual support and services, while also respecting the autonomy and distinctive character of each individual congregation. By 2014, JKI had grown to include 223 local churches located in nineteen Indonesian provinces and three other countries (United States, Netherlands, and Australia). Today, the JKI network numbers more than 400 congregations. Five of its congregations—Jakarta Praise Community Church (18,000 members), JKI Injil Kerajaan in Semarang (5,000), JKI Higher

Interior of the Holy Stadium in Semarang. PHOTOGRAPH COURTESY OF MENNONITE WORLD CONFERENCE

Than Ever in Semarang (5,000), JKI Bukit Zion in Surabaya (2,300), and JKI Maranatha in Ungaran-Semarang (1,850)— are among the largest churches in all of Indonesia.

So what is the glue that holds JKI together? What makes it attractive to the congregations who have become part of the synod? Clearly, it is not JKI's elaborate organizational structure—though the synod relies on the assistance of numerous volunteers, including a dozen or more area coordinators scattered across Indonesia, as of 2019, JKI had only five paid staff members. Nor does JKI's identity rest on carefully formulated theological statements. To be sure, the synod has established a Bible school—the Sangkakala STT (theological college) in Kopeng, Salatiga. The synod also oversees the ordination of pastors, and its Church Order outlines the basic expectations of each member church. Yet the non-denominational character of JKI, which consciously grants each member church the freedom to embody the gospel within its own particular context, is intentional and unmistakable.

A symbiotic relationship

JKI and its member churches relate symbiotically, with each contributing something vital to the other. Every JKI member church is encouraged to contribute 10 percent of their budget to the synod. In return, they receive several benefits, both tangible and spiritual. In the first place, JKI provides independent, nondenominational congregations with a legal status that would otherwise be nearly impossible for them to obtain in Indonesia. Within Indonesia's complex religious landscape, in which each citizen must declare themselves to be a member of an officially recognized religion, JKI's charter as a legally recognized synod has given it a coveted status within the nondenominational Christian community. If independent, charismatic congregations want to avoid the charge of being an illegal "sect," they need to have a church home. JKI provides that legal covering, along with the authority to ordain pastors, which is needed for these groups to operate legally.

Beyond that important pragmatic consideration, JKI also provides a spiritual home for nondenominational congregations who are not looking for a common confession of faith but who nonetheless seek fellowship with other groups who share certain affinities. When pressed on the question of a JKI theology, Eddy Suyanto, general secretary of JKI, insisted that "the fruit of your life is your theology."[113] But he also went on to identify five principles, or affinities, that one could expect to find in all JKI churches:

1. anointing of the Holy Spirit, with an openness to all the gifts of the Spirit, including speaking in tongues;

2. a commitment to evangelism and church growth;

3. a "theology of suffering and the cross," which implies that Christian faith entails sacrifice;

4. participation in home fellowships or cell groups; and

5. an expectation of material and spiritual blessing.

The charismatic authority of Adi Sutanto is clearly another important part of JKI's appeal. As the founder and father figure of the movement, Adi Sutanto is deeply respected among all JKI members. In the words of one JKI leader, "He is the father; the churches are his children. Like a family, this is a harmonious relationship; but the father is to be respected."

---

113. Eddy Suyanto, interview by author, Salatiga, Java, October 16, 2019.

Each year, JKI hosts two conferences that have become crucial to its ongoing identity. Every July, pastors and spouses from JKI member churches gather for several days of fellowship, inspiration, education, and encouragement. The primary focus of the annual JKI synod retreat is not on administrative agenda; rather, it functions more like a revival meeting, featuring inspiring worship led by well-known pastors and evangelists, combined with workshops, Bible studies, and special events for spouses, all in a setting conducive to relaxing in comfort.

In January, JKI hosts a similar event for leaders of groups who are not members of the synod. While this annual Workers in the Field of the Lord (KPLT) conference helps to elevate JKI's visibility within the broader Christian community, JKI leaders insist that the purpose is simply to bless all those who are involved in Christian ministry, with a special focus on leaders in small urban or rural churches who may feel isolated or in need of encouragement. In addition to the spiritual content, the January JKI conferences have become well-known in Indonesian Christian circles for the generous gifts that participants receive, ranging from rice makers and gas burners to computers and motorbikes.

The annual conferences are a reminder of JKI's Sangkakala origins as a charismatic renewal movement, while also serving to keep its member congregations connected and to maintain strong connections within the broader Christian community in Indonesia, which is still a small religious minority.

CHALLENGES FOR THE FUTURE

By all outward appearances, JKI is a thriving synod that has found a unique niche in the ecosystem of Indonesian Christianity. But like the GITJ and GKMI, it also faces some interesting challenges.

1. Naming and claiming its implicit theology

Although JKI leaders prefer to avoid conversations focused on the synod's theological identity, every group is shaped by a set of theological commitments, even if these convictions are not made explicit. In 1986, JKI created the Maranatha Theological Academy (Akademi Theologia Maranatha) in Ungaran to train future leaders for ministry. The school relocated to Kopeng, close to Salatiga, in 2002 as the Sangkakala Theological Seminary (STT Sangkakala). In 2019, the school had 190 students and offered both a four-year bachelor's degree and a master's program, with a vision of expanding to one thousand residential students and a much larger online presence.

Clearly, the teachers at the Sangkakala Bible School are shaping their courses around biblical themes that reflect *some* larger theological tradition, even if they are unaware of that tradition or do not explicitly name it. Textbooks and training materials, for example, all have an identifiable theological orientation; in a similar way, the JKI emphasis on the third person of the Trinity represents a *particular* lens for reading Scripture and applying Christ's teaching to daily life; and the JKI view of church polity is not shared by all Christian groups. The strong influence evident in some JKI congregations of Hillsong Worship music, or Christian Zionism, or a theology of "health and wealth," in addition to support for Anabaptist-Mennonite themes, all suggest that JKI will continue to sort out its theological identity in the coming years.

2. Balancing the spontaneity of the Spirit with strategic planning and cultural relevance

The JKI synod emerged from a context of charismatic renewal and a radical commitment to trust in the Spirit's leading and provision. Yet megachurches have enormous budgets to support their large staffs, market-sensitive programming, and sophisticated promotional campaigns. JKI congregations are closely attuned to the organizational language of goal setting, strategic planning, and rationalized systems of delivery. In such contexts, it can become very easy to overlook ways in which the medium shapes the message. And since delivering a highly polished message using the latest technology is expensive, the risk-taking vulnerability promised by the Spirit can be subtly replaced by the commercial pressures of maintaining market share in a competitive religious environment.

3. Keeping the Sangkakala vision alive

In a related way, all charismatic renewal movements face the challenge of passing along the energy and vibrancy of their founders to the next generation of believers. What will happen, for example, when Adi Sutanto is no longer present as the "father" of the JKI family?

As one response to this challenge, during the annual synod retreat in 2009, Adi Sutanto encouraged young leaders in the synod to convene JKI youth pastors and activists for a time of spiritual renewal. Led by Anton Kurniawan Sidharta and his wife, Lydia Adi (the daughter of Adi Sutanto), along with Yusup Rogo Yuono and Joshua Fibry, the leaders began to host a conference for the synod youth pastors called Unlimited Fire.

In 2006, the initiative expanded beyond JKI to connect with a much broader, interdenominational group of leaders. "Our goal," reflected Anton Kurniawan Sidharta, "is not to repeat what happened in 1979, but we want our generation to encounter God personally and powerfully today in ways that are relevant to young people."[114] Unlimited Fire has a strong presence on social media, and its programs reflect a clear understanding of the power of technology in its effort to strengthen networks among youth leaders in the various Indonesian Christian communities.

4. Balancing the charismatic presence of the Holy Spirit with social ministries . . . and political engagement

Churches that emphasize the charismatic gifts of the Spirit can easily focus their energies almost exclusively on the *experiential* dimensions of faith—worship filled with dancing, clapping, and amplified music; speaking in tongues; dramatic healings; or deliverance from demonic spirits. Pentecostal churches might have occasional campaigns to address social needs—a fundraiser after a natural disaster, for example—but they tend not to focus on social problems in a structural or systemic way. Many JKI churches, however, have challenged this stereotype, blending charismatic worship with truly impressive social ministries that speak to the physical and material needs of their communities as well as the spiritual.

The JKI Gospel of the Kingdom in Semarang—the megachurch that will host the MWC general assembly in 2022—is a great example of this holistic approach to ministry. Like most charismatic congregations, the worship services at JKI Gospel of the Kingdom are loud, colorful, and dynamic—participants arrive anticipating an encounter with the Holy Spirit. But, as noted, the church has also developed a remarkable range of social ministries—among other things, a soup kitchen, a clinic, legal aid for abused women, addictions counseling, sports programs,

---

114. Anton Kurniawan Sidharta, interview by author, September 21, 2019.

and an elementary/high school. These programs touch thousands of Semarang residents, including those who are not members of the congregation. And they are all the more remarkable given that Semarang is an overwhelmingly Muslim city.

This outreach is possible only because church leaders and key members have managed to nurture close relations with city and government officials. Given the long and complicated relationship between politics and religion in Indonesia, one ongoing challenge, especially for the megachurches in JKI, will be how to maintain a healthy balance between charismatic worship, vibrant social ministries, and the delicate political engagement that is needed to maintain such a visible, public presence in a Muslim-dominated culture.

WHERE THE SPIRIT LEADS

As the youngest of the three Indonesian synods that are members of Mennonite World Conference, JKI's identity is still in formation. The network of churches that form the synod has grown rapidly in the past ten to twenty years, and will likely continue to grow. Whether the Anabaptist-Mennonite connection that Adi Sutanto has encouraged will continue to be a significant part of the identity of the JKI will depend heavily on the next generation of leadership that emerges within the synod. Certainly the generous and gracious way that JKI leaders have supported the Mennonite World Conference general assembly points in a positive direction. And North American visitors to Indonesia who may find the worship style of JKI congregations to be overly exuberant should know that most visitors from other Mennonite World Conference churches in the global South are likely to feel right at home.

The Indonesian MWC Churches Today

IN JULY 2009, an unlikely group of church leaders from Indonesia found themselves in a conversation outside a dormitory in Asunción, Paraguay. Although the participants in the discussion were not strangers, their paths rarely crossed. The three Anabaptist-Mennonite synods they represented—the GITJ, GKMI, and JKI—had complex histories, each rooted in a particular set of memories that included stories of conflict and division.

But here in the relaxed context of the 15th general assembly of Mennonite World Conference, something significant shifted in their relationship. "At one particular moment," recalled David Meijanto, "we realized that all of us were of a similar age and that we shared many of the same concerns and values."[115] For the first time, members of the group asked an obvious question: "Why don't we get together more often back in Indonesia?"

---

115. John D. Roth, "Indonesian Churches to Host MWC Assembly in 2021," *The Mennonite* (April 2016), 9.

The church leaders returned to Indonesia with a commitment to meet every three months for the simple goal of sharing together and encouraging each other. At one of those "Inter-Menno" meetings not long thereafter, the idea emerged that the three synods could join together to host the 2021 MWC global assembly in Indonesia. Although the organizational task of managing the logistics for a gathering of thousands of people from all over the world was beyond the capacity of any single synod, perhaps the challenge would be manageable if all three would combine their efforts, especially if the Holy Stadium of the JKI Gospel of the Kingdom church in Semarang could serve as the primary venue.

After careful deliberation and prayer, the Inter-Menno group moved forward with a proposal to host the 2021 assembly. In 2012, the MWC General Council—the representative body of MWC's 107 members—accepted the invitation. Since then the Inter-Menno committee has been meeting regularly to plan the event, making adjustments, along with the rest of the world, due to the coronavirus pandemic by shifting the date a year forward so that the gathering will now be held in July 2022.

The conversations in 2009 that led to the formation of the Inter-Menno committee—and the hospitality that the three synods are collectively extending to the global Anabaptist-Mennonite church—mark a significant step in the long history of these churches.

As we have explored in these chapters, the three Anabaptist-Mennonite synods in Indonesia, born in the mid-nineteenth century out of a fusion of an indigenous Christian renewal movement led by Tunggul Wulung and the work of Dutch Mennonite missionaries, have faithfully embodied the good news of the gospel. Like every member group in MWC, they have been imperfect vessels. Each of the synods carries with it memories of conflict and pain—some of it a lingering legacy of encounters with European and North American Mennonites, some a result of ethnic prejudice and violence within Indonesia, and some a consequence of internal struggles within their own synods over resources, church polity, and leadership.

Yet each synod has also been entrusted with a treasure (2 Corinthians 4:7-9)—the liberating message of Jesus and the empowering presence of the Holy Spirit. And, in its own way, each group has flourished in recent decades, reaching out to the peoples and cultures around them in distinct and remarkably effective ways.

As the GITJ, GKMI, and JKI synods look to the future, they face a host of exciting challenges. Many of these challenges—the degradation of the environment and the growing climate crisis, the persistence of racial and ethnic prejudices, and divisions along economic lines, for example—are shared, in one form or another, by virtually every other MWC member church. Yet even if the general nature of the challenges ahead are familiar to many groups, the shared context of culture, politics, and history among the GITJ, GKMI, and JKI synods provides unique opportunities in the coming years to address those challenges together, perhaps in the same collaborative spirit that has made it possible for them to host the 17th MWC general assembly. Four themes, in particular, are likely to dominate the attention of the Anabaptist-Mennonite synods of Indonesia.

1. CHRISTIAN IDENTITY IN A MULTIRELIGIOUS CONTEXT

As we have seen, Indonesia has long been home to a wide variety of religious groups, including all the world's major religions. To a remarkable degree, the religions that have flourished in

Indonesia have been tolerant of each other, even syncretic, fluidly absorbing some aspects of neighboring faiths along with elements of an indigenous Indonesian animism that has persisted well into the twenty-first century.

Yet within this diverse context there is no escaping the fact that Islam is the overwhelmingly dominant religion in Indonesia today, as it has been for several centuries. Islam is clearly a cultural and political force in Indonesia. Islamic mosques, cultural centers, and religious schools are visible almost everywhere in Indonesia. Even though Indonesia is officially a secular state, with its constitution guaranteeing freedom of worship to six of the world's major religions, in most sectors of Indonesian society clear advantages—legal or not—accrue to those who are Muslim. And in some areas of the country, militant forms of Islam are gaining ground over the more relaxed, syncretistic expressions that have traditionally dominated Indonesia.

This means that Christians in Indonesia—as in many other countries in the global South—must forge their identity as a religious minority, and that Christian-Muslim relationships will remain an unavoidable priority.

This is not new. Christians and Muslims in Indonesia have lived and worked alongside each other for centuries, and they have generally found creative ways to accommodate each other's presence. At the same time, it can sometimes feel as if the accommodation moves mostly in one direction: the official Indonesian calendar is highly attentive to Muslim religious holidays; there is no escaping the loudspeakers calling Muslims to prayer five times every day; Christians often stop their work on Fridays between 11:30 a.m. and 1:30 p.m. for the Muslim worship and are required to work on Sunday; and Christians generally refrain from eating pork so as not to offend their Muslim neighbors. In some localities, Christians have faced enormous difficulties in securing permits to buy land or to build churches. Some have faced significant discrimination in the workforce. And in the most extreme cases, Christians—especially those who are ethnic Chinese—have periodically experienced waves of horrific violence that have left them physically and emotionally traumatized.[116]

To a degree that is difficult for many outsiders to fully appreciate, members of the Indonesian Anabaptist-Mennonite synods have given enormous creative thought to questions associated with religious pluralism. Each synod would describe itself as fully committed to evangelism; with GKMI and JKI quite vigorous in promoting their missional identity. Yet all the synods are extremely sensitive in their approach to evangelism in Muslim contexts.

Many narratives of Muslim conversion involve a supernatural experience of some sort—a vivid dream, a miraculous healing, an angelic visitation—in which the agent of conversion is not another Christian but the intervention of the Holy Spirit. If a Muslim does make a profession of Christian faith, it may be a very long time before that person submits to public baptism, since the familial and social costs of formally leaving the Islamic community are often extremely high. Sometimes a Muslim will participate for a long time in a Christian house fellowship while still worshiping at the mosque. Nor would it be uncommon to see women wearing the Muslim head covering (hijab) while attending a JKI youth rally. Few Anabaptist-Mennonite pastors in Indonesia would demand that new

---

116. For several examples of these challenges, see Stefanus Christian Haryono, "Mennonite History and Identity in Indonesia," *Mission Focus: Annual Review* 9 (2001): 67–68.

believers officially change their religion on their identity card, recognizing the economic, social, and political costs that such a decision would likely entail, though, in time, many converts choose to do so.[117]

Although the threat of religious violence, though exceedingly rare these days, is never completely gone from the equation, I have never heard a church leader describe Muslims as enemies who are utterly lost souls, or declare with the certainty of many conservative Christians in the West that Muslims and Christians do not worship the same God. And the challenge of balancing confident witness with appropriate cultural sensitivity and creative accommodation is never fully resolved. Given the tendency among many Christians in the West to regard Islam only through the lens of its most extreme and militant form, the nuanced complexity of Christian-Muslim relationships in Indonesia, forged out of decades of practical experience at the local level, has much to teach us.

2. ANABAPTIST-MENNONITE IDENTITY IN AN ECUMENICAL CONTEXT

As a very small minority, Christians in Indonesia have not generally invested a great deal of energy into sharpening doctrinal or denominational differences. Clearly, the Reformed Church has a dominant presence within the Indonesian Christian community—one legacy of the Dutch colonial presence. And other missions, among them Lutherans, Baptists, Salvation Army, and Seventh-day Adventists, have also imparted their

---

117. By law, the identity card required of every Indonesian citizen must include a declaration of religious affiliation with one of the six officially recognized religions. Even though Indonesia officially affirms the freedom of religion, the social costs of conversion in some parts of the country—especially from Islam to Christianity— can be very high.

denominational identities to the churches that emerged from their efforts.

But since the middle of the nineteenth century, various Christian ecumenical organizations—regional and national— have emerged in Indonesia, and have generally enjoyed a great deal of support as Javanese Christians from various denominations have long collaborated on hymnbooks, theological schools, Sunday school curricula, and revival campaigns. This impulse toward ecumenism might also be regarded as a natural extension of a deep cultural history of multireligious accommodation.

Adding to the muted denominational identity of churches in Indonesia is a cultural tendency to honor the leadership of respected individuals, whose authority is often passed from one generation to the next. This means that the identity of individual congregations is sometimes associated with personal loyalty to a charismatic or wise leader more than with the larger theological or denominational tradition to which congregational identity nominally belongs. Relations between congregations and the synod—where denominational identity is generally nurtured—have been fraught.

All of these factors come into play when asking about the Anabaptist-Mennonite identity of the congregations who are part of the GITJ, GKMI, or JKI. Clearly, the sustained encounter with missionaries from the Dutch Mennonite Mission Society in the late nineteenth and early twentieth century, followed by the influential presence of various European and North American mission and relief agencies in the difficult years after World War II, played a significant role in the theological formation of the synods. Key leaders in each of the synods have had significant contact with Mennonite Central

Committee, the European Mennonite Mission Committee, and Mennonite World Conference. Both the International Volunteer Exchange Program (IVEP) and the Young Anabaptist Mennonite Exchange Network (YAMEN!) have enabled scores of Indonesian young people to encounter Anabaptist-Mennonite groups in other countries, broadening their exposure to the wider theological tradition.

In the past two decades several synod leaders, especially in the GKMI, have made a sustained and conscious effort to introduce congregations to key aspects of Anabaptist history and theology. In the aftermath of the renewed ethnic violence in 1998, numerous GKMI churches introduced into their public spaces images from the *Martyrs Mirror* of sixteenth-century Anabaptist martyrs. Dutch Anabaptist Dirk Willems saving his would-be captor from drowning, for example, is part of a stained glass window in the GKMI Winong congregation in Pati. GKMI congregations recite the well-known saying from the Anabaptist Hans Denck ("No one can truly know Christ unless they follow him in life") as part of their regular Sunday liturgy, and in many GKMI and GITJ congregations the language of reconciliation and peacebuilding has become an integral part of pastoral formation and public identity.

In addition, several historians—among them Heru Sigit Sukoco, Alle Hoekema, Adhi Dharma, and Lawrence Yoder—have made a significant contribution to a stronger sense of ecclesial identity through the publication of several detailed histories of the GITJ and the GKMI. Still, it is probably safe to say that relatively few members at the congregational level—perhaps especially in the case of JKI, with its strong orientation as a safe haven for nondenominational churches—would quickly identify themselves with the Anabaptist-Mennonite tradition, or even know what those words meant.[118]

As historian Adhi Dharma has noted, "Mennonitism does not have deep roots in Indonesian culture, society or politics; and Christianity itself still can have something of a negative connotation, given its close association with Western colonialism."[119] So the bigger challenge remains that of contextualizing Anabaptist-Mennonite values within the Indonesian context.

3. INTER-MENNONITE COLLABORATION DESPITE MEMORIES OF DIVISION

Despite these strong impulses to affirm religious pluralism and Christian ecumenicity, the Indonesian Anabaptist-Mennonite synods—like most other churches who are part of Mennonite World Conference—also share a long history of conflict and division.

Each specific conflict, of course, has a narrative of its own, often shaped by local circumstances and the personalities involved. But the deeper sources of those divisions are painfully familiar to Anabaptist-Mennonites from around the world: tensions over church polity, authority, and leadership; disputes regarding finances and access to resources; prejudices rooted in ethnic or linguistic identity; and the basic human tendency to

118. A significant exception to this would be the three JKI congregations in the Los Angeles area (JKI Anugerah, Indonesian Worship Church, and International Christian Community Fellowship) who were received as members of the Franconia Mennonite Conference (now Mosaic) in 2017, culminating a ten-year relationship. The Conference also has strong connections with two Indonesian-speaking congregations in Philadelphia—the Nations Worship Center and Philadelphia Praise Center.

119. Adhi Dharma, "Indonesia: Struggling, Learning, Serving," *MWC Courier* (Oct. 2013), 15.

divide over politics, education, class, and personality—and all these have been part of GITJ, GKMI, and JKI history.

Very few individuals or groups find it easy to openly acknowledge the conflict that has been part of their past. This natural reluctance to address conflict is compounded in the Indonesian cultural context, which places a high value on social harmony, or at least its outward appearance. Both Javanese and Bahasa Indonesian, for example, are rich with sayings and aphorisms that are useful for communicating in highly indirect ways. Courtesy may require someone in Indonesia to say yes to avoid a direct confrontation, while in reality, what seemed like agreement is just the opposite. It is not quite accurate to simply dismiss these cultural habits as unhealthy expressions of "conflict avoidance"; in many instances, they can helpfully curb the impulse to speak rashly, thereby avoiding regret for the damage caused by an intemperate comment.

But even with all of these cultural guardrails in place, there is no denying that conflict is part of the human condition. In settings where direct confrontation is very hard, small grievances and slights can fester for a long time. And when the suppressed conflict spills out into acts of mob violence directed against a specific group of people—as was the case in Indonesia in the 1940s, the early 1960s, and again in 1998—the trauma can become generational.

In many ways, the synods today have moved beyond the antagonisms that separated them in the past, as well as beyond the conflicts that have divided them from within. The debates in both the GITJ and GKMI over the ownership of schools, hospitals, and other church properties, for example—debates that tore the synods apart in the 1980s and 1990s—are mostly a distant memory for younger pastors and church leaders.

In the 1980s, the circumstances around the emergence of the JKI deeply divided some families and friends, as some chose to remain within the GKMI. But it would appear that most of those wounds are now healed. Earlier resentments against the Dutch Mission or Mennonite Central Committee have largely been healed. And basic questions of polity—the debates over the authority of the congregation versus the authority of the synod that once festered in the GITJ and GKMI synods—have been mostly resolved.

Still, like all groups with a complicated history, the GITJ, GKMI, and JKI will need to continue to nurture these positive relationships by tending to new forms of cooperation and collaboration that can help liberate them from the impulse to act out the painful memories and established stereotypes of the past. The remarkable steps church leaders have taken to form Inter-Menno, and the courage they have expressed in agreeing to collaborate as hosts of the 17th MWC general assembly, point to a new chapter in their history.

4. HONORING ELDERS WHILE INTEGRATING YOUNG PEOPLE

Like many countries in the global South, the demographics of Indonesia today are heavily skewed toward young people: 42 percent of the Indonesian population is under the age of twenty-five. This means that all three synods face the challenge of reaching out to a highly mobile generation of young people in order to integrate them into the life of the church.

Negotiating successful transitions from one generation to the next is a challenge for every group, of course, but the difficulties are heightened in an Indonesian culture that traditionally honors age, seniority, and established authority figures. These cultural tendencies, combined with a long history of dependence within the church on European and North American financial support, can encourage a posture of passivity among lay members, while also sowing the seeds for discontent among gifted young people who are not well integrated into the leadership structures and are frustrated when their gifts go untapped. Certainly all the synods—particularly JKI—are attentive to these dynamics. But the cultural realities are still there.

The list of future challenges could go on. In the end, the challenges themselves are familiar—it is only the Indonesian context within which these challenges are unfolding that is unique.

One of the many blessings of being part of a global church is the opportunity cross-cultural encounters provide for each group to recognize familiar themes that bind us all together, as well as the distinctive cultures that call each of us to the hard, creative, and joyful work of discernment. So it is with the history of the GITJ, GKMI, and JKI synods—their stories, like visits to foreign lands, are filled with much that seems distant and strange; yet the closer we look, the more it becomes apparent that we are indeed brothers and sisters of a common family, faced with similar threats, empowered by similar spiritual resources, and called to walk the journey together with compassion, hospitality, and generosity.

A (Very Brief!) Travel Guide to Indonesia

*I*NDONESIA IS HOME to an amazing diversity of natural beauty, sites of historical interest, cultural treasures, and culinary delights. For fuller information on a much wider range of travel options in Indonesia, consider purchasing a travel guide (e.g., Fodor's, Lonely Planet, Budget Travel, Baedeker). What follows here are a few details that might be helpful for those attending the 17th Mennonite World Conference Global Assembly, and anyone who is interested in exploring sites relevant to the MWC-related churches in Java today.

INFORMATION SPECIFIC TO MENNONITE WORLD CONFERENCE

1. The MWC 17th Global Assembly in Semarang (July 2022) will include a range of gatherings:

   - Global Youth Summit, organized by the Young Anabaptists, or YABs (Salatiga, July 1–4, 2022)

- MWC General Council business meeting of MWC member church representatives
- MWC Executive Committee
- four MWC Commissions (Faith and Life; Deacons; Mission; and Peace)
- MWC Networks (Mission; Service; Peace)
- three new MWC Networks that are just emerging (Health; Primary School Educators; Secondary School Educators)
- Global Assembly: worship, singing, workshops/seminars
- Assembly Scattered: opportunities to travel with other assembly participants to visit local congregations and tourist sites

2. The primary venue for the event is the "Holy Stadium" of the JKI Gospel of the Kingdom (JKI Injil Kerajaan), located close to the airport in the bustling Central Javanese city of Semarang.

3. Semarang has a new, efficient airport. A common itinerary for flights from North America would be to arrive in Jakarta or Singapore, with a connecting flight to Semarang. MWC personnel will be at the Semarang airport to assist in transitioning to lodging and the Assembly site.

4. Be sure to register for the MWC Global Assembly prior to arrival. The assembly website (mwc-cmm.org/assembly/indonesia-2022) provides a daily schedule as well as options for workshops/seminars, lodging, and Assembly Scattered tours organized by MWC.

5. The theme of the 17th Global Assembly is "Following Jesus together across barriers." The morning worship service will feature vibrant music, a teaching on one aspect of the theme, and updates from various aspects of MWC's work. Participants will then have opportunities to participate in a wide range of workshops, seminars, service projects, and discussion groups. Each evening, participants will regather for another time of worship and celebration.

6. Assembly Scattered Tours: The MWC Assembly staff in Indonesia has organized a wonderful variety of short (one- to five-day) excursions—some available before the assembly and some afterward—that give participants the opportunity to visit local GITJ, GKMI, or JKI churches, learn more about their history, and see tourist sites in the area. This will be the simplest way to make additional connections to the people and sites in Central Java.

A BRIEF TOUR OF CENTRAL JAVA: SITES OF SPECIAL INTEREST TO THE MWC SYNODS OF INDONESIA

Jakarta: The Indonesian capital city of Jakarta is located on the western edge of Java, the archipelago's central, and most densely populated, island. Although there are JKI and GKMI congregations in Jakarta, most Anabaptist-Mennonite historical sites and the primary centers of the three synods today are located in Central Java, with the largest concentration of churches situated in the northern coastal region around a dormant volcano known as Mount Muria.

Semarang: Most people attending the MWC assembly will arrive in Semarang, a rapidly growing port city on the north-central coast whose new, modern airport is located very close to the JKI Holy Stadium. Semarang is an old Dutch administrative center and the provincial capital of Central Java. The Outstadt (Dutch for "old city") is full of slowly decaying colonial-era buildings. Semarang is also Indonesia's most Chinese city, featuring the Sam Po Kong Buddhist temple, built in honor of Admiral Cheng Ho, a Muslim eunuch of the Ming dynasty who led the Chinese fleet on numerous expeditions to Java and other parts of Indonesia in the early fifteenth century. Another famous landmark is the Lawang Sewu (Thousand Doors)—two enormous colonial buildings that were formerly the headquarters of the Indonesia railroad and then repurposed into a notorious center for interrogation during the Japanese occupation of 1942–1945. The classical Tay Kak Sie temple, built in the middle of the eighteenth century, is also impressive. The temple is close to a well-known Chinese food court (Pujasera Tay Yak Sie) that also features a model of the ships used by Cheng Ho. The GITJ, GKMI, and JKI all have congregations in Semarang. The newest congregation—the JKI Higher Than Ever megachurch—formed when the JKI Gospel of the Kingdom divided after the death of its pastor, Petrus Agung, in 2016.

Salatiga: Directly south of Semarang, some fifty kilometers (thirty miles) by car, is the town of Salatiga. A former Dutch trading post, the city continues to be an important commercial city connecting Semarang with Surakarta. Located just outside Salatiga, not far from the Satya Wacana Christian University, is the JKI Sangkakala Theological Seminary—site of the MWC Global Youth Summit—along with the offices of the JKI synod. Salatiga is also home to several JKI congregations, including JKI Keluarga Kerajaan and several GKMI congregations.

The offices of IndoMenno—an organization that emerged after MCC was forced to leave the country—are also in Salatiga.

Kudus (Arabic *al-Quds*, meaning Jerusalem): Heading east from Semarang brings you to Kudus, a significant town in the history of the GKMI. Established by Muslim saint Sunan Kudus, the city is a Muslim pilgrimage site, but it also has strong links to Hinduism (slaughter of cows is forbidden in the region). Kudus is famous for its printing industry, tobacco warehouses, and cigarette production—with more than two dozen factories—including the well-known clove cigarettes (*Kretek*). Ninety percent of the cigarettes produced in Indonesia come from Kudus. The town is also noted for several culinary specialties, including *Jenang Kudus*—a candy made of rice, brown sugar, and coconut—and *Soto Kudus*, a rich chicken soup with garlic and turmeric. Kudus was the home of Tee Siem Tat, founder of the GKMI church in the 1920s. Two of the largest GKMI churches in Java are located here, along with a large, well-equipped, GKMI-owned hospital (Rumah Sakit Mardi Rahayu). If you get to Kudus, be sure to check out the remarkable stained glass windows of the GKMI Kudus church, designed by Charles Christano, and the way in which the congregation has preserved an architectural memory of its first church house. A sister congregation, GKMI Rayon 2, also has a beautiful church in the city.

Kayuapu: Just north of the main road that heads out of Kudus, at the southern foot of Mount Muria, a short detour will bring you to Kayuapu, home of GITJ Kayuapu. In the 1850s, a Reformed congregation emerged here under the leadership of missionary W. Hoezoo of Dutch Missionary Fellowship. Pasrah

Noeriman became an important Javanese leader in the Kayuapu congregation. In 1898 this congregation came under the care of the Dutch Mennonite Mission, along with a school and clinic. A cemetery associated with the GITJ Kayuapu includes the gravesite of Pieter and Wilhelmina Jansz.

Pati: Continuing east on the main road out of Kudus, now with Mount Muria looming to the north, you will arrive at Pati. If Salatiga is the administrative center of the JKI synod and Kudus the home of the GKMI, Pati is home to the synod offices of the GITJ. The GITJ's Wiyata Wacana Theological College is in Pati, along with three GITJ congregations, several government-supported schools for training teachers of Christianity in the public schools, and several Christian schools loosely associated with the synod. The offices of the Inter-Mennonite Scholarship Foundation and Development Commission are located in the building on Penjawi Street that once served as Mennonite Central Committee headquarters for Indonesia. During the late 1960s and 1970s, the Pati congregation of the GITJ led the way in fostering the formation of new congregations. At least ten of its branch congregations came to maturity during that period. The GKMI Winong-Pati congregation, formed about 1940, has also been instrumental in planting several congregations in the surrounding area, as well as a branch church on the island of Sumatra.

Tayu: Heading north toward the coast, skirting the east flank of Mount Muria, is Tayu. In the late 1920s, Tayu became the center of a great deal of Mennonite Mission activity focused especially on medical care. The Tayu Mission Hospital, once an imposing building, supported numerous branch clinics throughout the Muria region. In 1942, a group of young local Muslims, emboldened by the Japanese occupation of Indonesia, burned the hospital and many of the buildings associated with it. The church recovered, however, and GITJ Tayu remains an active congregation.

Banyutowo/Margorejo [Puncel, Dukuhseti, Pati Regency]: Continuing around the coastline north of Tayu northeast of Mount Muria, you will arrive at GITJ Banyutowo, a congregation established in 1861 by Tunggul Wulung, a Javanese mystic and Christian evangelist who worked alongside the Mennonite Mission. Tunggul Wulung had a vision to create agricultural settlements for new Javanese Christians that would integrate their economic, social, and religious lives in settings that were free from the Dutch compulsory labor laws and isolated from the dominant Muslim community. One of the first of these settlements emerged at Banyutowo. Only a few miles away is the GITJ Margorejo congregation, site of another agricultural settlement, modeled after Tunggul Wulung's vision, that Pieter Anthonie Jansz established in 1881 on behalf of the Dutch Mennonite Mission. The Margorejo settlement eventually included a mission school, a teacher training school, and a clinic. On August 12, 1929, Roeben Martoredjo, a lay evangelist in the Margorejo congregation, became the first Javanese pastor to be ordained by the Mennonite Mission.

Donorojo: Driving farther north along the coast will bring you to the GITJ Donorojo church, located close to the ruins of an old Portuguese fort. The leprosy village of Donorojo, located next to the church, was opened in 1916 as an extension of the hospital in nearby Kelet. The name Donorojo means "gift of the queen," since much of the funding came from the Netherlands in honor of Queen Wilhelmina on the birth of her daughter Juliana. The church, designed by the Lutheran medical doctor Karl Gramberg, includes beautiful stained glass windows and a special section to seat people from the leprosy village next to it.

Bondo: Home of Tunggul Wulung's first agricultural community, Ujung Watu, established close to the sea in 1856, and site of his gravestone. The Mennonite Mission established a similar settlement (1898) in nearby **Margokerto**. Southeast of **Mlonggo**—a farming village of nearly 600 households, almost all of whom are Christians—is Cumbring, the site of the former Soekias plantation where Pieter Jansz first worked as a teacher after his arrival in 1851. The GITJ **Bondo** congregation is south of Margokerto. Several miles farther south will bring you to the GITJ **Kedungpenjalin** church where Pasrah Karso—another Javanese evangelist and contemporary of Tunggul Wulung—was a central figure in the early history of the congregation. Groups associated with Tunggul Wulung and Pasrah Karso eventually merged with the Mennonite Mission, accounting for most of the early growth in the mission effort.

Jepara: The seaside town of Jepara is famous throughout Indonesia for its traditional wood carving and handcrafted furniture, with the main center for this artisanal work located some three kilometers (two miles) south of Jepara in the village of Tahunan. Although the GITJ synod offices are in Pati, Jepara—and the region around it—is the historical home of the GITJ. The large GITJ Jepara congregation features beautiful wood carvings along with a painting of the Gunungan, a leaf-shaped image familiar in traditional Javanese theater that has been reconceived here in a Christian context as a representation of the cosmos. Right next to the GITJ Jepara congregation is a large artisanal shop, owned by a member of the congregation, that features a wide range of local crafts.

If you spend time in Jepara, consider a visit to **Karimunjawa Islands**, a marine national park made of numerous white sand islands with beautiful swimming and snorkeling, marine life, and coral reefs.

FREQUENTLY ASKED QUESTIONS

What language is spoken in Indonesia? Will I be able to get around using English?

Most Indonesians do not speak English. Even in cities, there is no guarantee that you will be able to speak English in every setting. The language, which is almost universally understood across the country, is Bahasa Indonesian. It would be a good idea to familiarize yourself with some basic phrases (see page 180). You can also learn simple Indonesian expressions from the monthly MWC Indonesian language video series at https://mwc-cmm.org/resources/learning-indonesian-language.

Do I need to apply for a visa, or will I be able to enter the country with my passport?

If you are traveling as a tourist with a U.S. or Canadian passport, you do not need a visa to enter Indonesia as long as you are staying for fewer than thirty days. If you wish to stay longer than thirty days, you must apply for a thirty-day visa upon arrival, which you may then extend by an additional thirty days at the immigration office in Indonesia. It is important that your passport is valid for at least six months from the date of your arrival in Indonesia, and that you have at least two blank pages in your passport. Immigration authorities take these regulations very seriously, and you will be denied entry if your passport does not fulfill these requirements.

What is the weather like?

Summer in Indonesia is hot. Temperatures in June and July average 80°F (26°C) and the humidity usually hovers around 75 percent. You can expect very little rain—it is likely that there will be none at all.

What clothes should I pack?

The majority of the country is Muslim, and most people you see will be dressed in a fairly conservative style. You should avoid low necklines and short shorts or short skirts. If you want to visit a temple, you should plan to wear loose-fitting clothing with sleeves that cover your shoulders, and pants that extend below the knee. Women should also expect to cover their hair. The climate is tropical, so light and comfortable material is advised. Many Indonesians will wear sandals in informal situations—for tourists, sandals or comfortable shoes are a sensible option. Avoid wearing flashy or expensive jewelry, as it may attract pickpockets.

What kind of electrical outlets does Indonesia use?

If you are traveling from the United States or Canada, you may need both a wall plug adapter and voltage converter. Outlets in Indonesia are type C and F—commonly known as the European outlet. A voltage converter is necessary, as the standard voltage in Indonesia (230 V) is higher than the standard in the United States and devices can be seriously damaged if they are charged without a converter. Many outlet adapters also function as a voltage converter—be sure to check when you are purchasing your adapter to make sure that it has the features you want. You can find adapters and converters online, as well as pieces that function as both.

The frequency in Indonesia (50 Hz) also differs from that of the United States and Canada (60 Hz). Not all devices require frequency conversion, but you can check the label on your device to be sure. If it says "INPUT: 100–240 V, 50/60 Hz," it may be used without a converter. This is common in most chargers (laptops, phones, tablets, cameras, toothbrushes, etc.), so you probably don't need to use a converter with these devices.

Should I plan to bring sunscreen or bug spray?

It is a good idea to bring sunscreen and use it judiciously. It can be difficult to find sunscreen to purchase, and it can be expensive. You should plan to use bug repellant of some kind. You may bring your own, but it is also possible to buy in the city. Many people use a spray, but other popular options include repellent bracelets and wall plug-ins.

What are bathrooms like in Indonesia?

Although tourist areas often have Western-style toilets, most Indonesian toilets are squat toilets—essentially holes in the bathroom floor. There may be a handle to flush the toilet, but it is more common to flush by using a small scoop-like device (called *gayung*) located in a bucket or tank next to the toilet, and pouring the water into the toilet. This same scoop is used for cleanup in the style of a bidet—most public bathrooms do not provide toilet paper. Some bathrooms include a hose with a spray nozzle, which serves the same purpose. Many tourists choose to carry toilet paper with them, and there will usually be a bucket to collect used toilet tissue. Do not flush toilet paper, as it can cause issues in the sewer systems, which are generally not built to handle paper waste.

What can I do to travel in an ecologically responsible way?

Environmental care is not a high priority for most Indonesians, but there are still ways to try to limit your ecological footprint as a tourist.

- Demand for water is often greater than supply. You should try to conserve water in whatever ways you can, including taking short showers, turning off the tap when you do not need it, and avoiding places with pools.

- Drinking bottled water is recommended for your health, but also leads to high levels of plastic waste. Depending on where you are staying, it may be possible to refill a reusable bottle from large containers of drinking water. You can ask if this is an option.

- Conserve power by turning off your lights whenever possible. An even bigger issue is air conditioning, which you should use judiciously.

- Consider taking public transportation instead of hiring a taxi or renting a car. Public buses in Semarang charge 3,000Rp per trip. You will also have the option of taking a *becak*—Indonesia's three-wheeled, pedal-powered bike with a passenger seat. Short becak rides generally cost about 5,000Rp, and longer ones about 10,000Rp. Be sure to agree on the cost before the ride begins.

What about money?

Indonesia uses the rupiah. In early 2021, the exchange rate was about 14,400Rp to one dollar. In most locations, you should not have a problem finding an ATM or using a credit card. Tipping is not mandatory, though some restaurants and hotels will include a service charge automatically. If you would like to tip, you may add 5 to 10 percent of the total bill.

What about food?

Food varies greatly across Indonesia, but is delicious in every setting! In Java, steamed rice is a staple and is served with every meal. Rice can be cooked in coconut milk or colored yellow with turmeric. Dried cassava, noodles, or potatoes are often served along with rice. For snacks between meals, you might encounter yam, taro, and sweet potatoes. Vegetables are also an important part of Javanese cuisine, and plates are often flavored with shallots, garlic, turmeric, ginger, and chili. Freshwater fish such as carp, tilapia, and catfish are popular, and seafood like tuna, shrimp, squid, and salted fish are often served in coastal cities. Meat in Java usually consists of chicken, goat, beef, and mutton. Pork is not typically served, as a high percentage of Javanese are Muslim.

What religions will I encounter in Indonesia?

An overwhelming majority of Indonesians consider religion to be essential—some form of religion is present in almost all aspects of society, including politics, education, marriage, and public holidays. Indonesia is a predominantly Muslim country, which means that you will hear public calls to prayer through-out the day, from very early in the morning until late at night. The landscape—both rural and urban—is dotted with mosques and Muslim community or cultural centers. Like Christianity, the Islamic faith in Indonesia has many different expressions, so don't assume that all Muslims you encounter are alike! Almost 11 percent of Indonesians are Christians; others may be Hindu, Buddhist, or of other traditions. The strongest concentration of Hinduism is in the island of Bali; most Buddhists in Indonesia are of Chinese descent.

Can I drink the water?

No, you should probably not drink the tap water. Bottled water is easily available and typically quite cheap. Even better, refill your own water bottle at the water stations you will see in most hotel lobbies or public buildings. Most ice in restaurants is safe, as long as it looks uniform in shape—this is usually an indicator that the ice comes from a manufacturing plant. You should avoid ice that has been chipped off a larger block.

If I am planning to travel before or after my visit, what is the easiest way to arrange my travel?

1. **Information:** The Internet offers an amazing set of resources for people who enjoy putting together their own travel packages. In addition to numerous one- to three-day excursions that you can find at local Indonesian travel agencies, you can also plan your own trip by exploring various sites online. For example, Indonesia's official tourism website, Wonderful Indonesia (www.indonesia.travel), is a great place to explore travel possibilities, including sites that are off the beaten path. You can also work with well-known printed travel guides such as Lonely Planet, Insight Guide, and Baedeker.

2. **Travel within Indonesia:** For tourists, the most common way to travel between islands is via airplane. Major airlines offer frequent service to connecting islands like Java, Bali, and Sumatra, but you can access many other islands via small chartered aircraft. The national ferry system, the Pelayaran Nasional Indonesia—commonly known as "Pelni"—is another easy way to navigate the Indonesian islands. The boats typically have quality service and good amenities; there are few places you won't be able to reach by this method of travel.

3. **Lodging:** Indonesia has quite a range of lodging options, but the three types of accommodation that you are most likely to utilize are hotels, private villas, or homestays. Mid-range hotels abound in Indonesia and can be fairly basic, but almost always have private bathrooms with a shower and toilet as well as a ceiling fan or perhaps air conditioning, all for a very reasonable price. At the lower end of the hotel spectrum you can expect just a mattress to sleep on and a *mandi*-style bathroom (with squat toilets and bucket showers) shared with other guests. Major chains accept credit cards for payment, but at smaller hotels you'll be expected to pay in rupiah. You will find many options for hotels in Indonesia through the standard websites, but you can sometimes find better deals by booking through niche hotel sites that cater to the Indonesian or Asian market (such as KlikHotel.com).

A FEW BASIC WORDS/PHRASES IN BAHASA INDONESIAN

Hello	*Salam*
How are you?	*Apa kabar?*
Excuse me	*Permisi*
Sorry	*Maaf*
Please	*Silahkan*
Thank you	*Terima kasih*
Yes	*Ya*
No	*Tidak*
My name is . . .	*Nama saya . . .*
Where is [the] . . . ?	*Di mana . . . ?*
How much is it . . . ?	*Berapa . . . ?*
Is there . . . [e.g., a toilet]?	*Ada . . . ?*
I need . . .	*Saya perlu . . .*
restroom	*kamar kecil*
toilet	*toilet*
bicycle/rickshaw	*becak*
bus	*bis*
minibus	*bemo*
taxi	*taksi*

Public signs

Buka	Open
Dilarang	Prohibited
Kamar Kecil	Restrooms
Keluar	Exit
Masuk	Entrance
Pria	Men
Wanitai	Women
Tutup	Closed

Recipes to Try at Home

*G*IVEN THE DIVERSITY of ethnic groups and cultures that have shaped Indonesian history, it is not surprising that Indonesians today enjoy a wide range of food. Yet within the diversity of Indonesian cuisine, one consistent theme is the rich variety of complex flavors that are guaranteed to delight your taste buds. Indonesians tend to enjoy hot and spicy food, often seasoned with a chili sauce known as *sambal*. But even if you don't like spicy foods, Indonesian dishes almost always combine basic flavors—sweet, salty, even sour—in creative ways that never cease to surprise. In my experience, street food in Java is both inexpensive and delicious. The recipes below—most of them provided by friends from the JKI, GKMI, or GITJ synods—may not replicate the full authenticity of Indonesian street food. But they will at least point you in the direction of the flavors and aromas that help to make Indonesian cuisine so special.

Indonesian Fried Rice (Nasi Goreng)

This spicy rice mix is a standard dish in Indonesia. Usually this fried rice is served with sambal (spicy relish) and prawn crackers.

Ingredients

12 ounces long-grain white rice
3 cups water
Salt, to taste
2 tablespoons sunflower seed oil
1 pound skinless, boneless chicken breast halves, chopped into 1-inch pieces
2 cloves garlic, coarsely chopped
1 fresh red chile pepper, seeded and chopped
1 tablespoon curry paste
1 bunch green onions, thinly sliced
2 tablespoons soy sauce, or more to taste
1 teaspoon sunflower seed oil
2 eggs
2 ounces roasted peanuts, coarsely chopped
¼ cup chopped fresh cilantro

Instructions

1. Bring rice, water, and salt to a boil in a saucepan. Reduce heat to medium-low, cover, and simmer until rice is tender and liquid has been absorbed, about 20–25 minutes.

2. Heat 2 tablespoons sunflower oil in a wok or skillet over medium-high heat; cook and stir chicken, garlic, and red chili pepper until chicken is golden brown, 5–7 minutes. Stir in curry paste and cook until fragrant, about 1 minute. Add cooked rice and green onions, cooking and stirring for 5 minutes more. Season with soy sauce.

3. Push rice mixture to one side of the wok. Heat remaining 1 teaspoon sunflower oil in the middle of wok; cook and stir eggs until just set, about 1 minute. Stir rice mixture into eggs. Sprinkle with peanuts and cilantro. Serve immediately.

Steamed Salted Duck Egg (Botok Telur Asin) Injil Kerajaan

Victoria Christine and Lena Kumalasari (JKI Maranatha)

PHOTOGRAPH COURTESY OF VICTORIA CHRISTINE

This is a traditional meal from Java Island. The word botok *refers to dishes wrapped in banana leaves, which can also be used in tofu or mushroom recipes. My family and I love to have botok telur asin. We add sweet soy sauce to balance the flavor and eat it with warm rice. It has a delicious savory and fresh taste, with the green tomatoes just the right bit of sourness. It tastes best if it's spicy!*

Salted duck eggs, which have been brined in salt for several weeks, can be found in Asian markets. You will need raw, not cooked eggs. Chicken eggs can be substituted, but the taste and texture will be different, and you may need to use more eggs—instructions to brine your own eggs can be found online.

You may also want to watch videos to see how to fill and fold the banana leaves. Alternatively, layer small stainless steel bowls with banana leaves and place the bowls in the steamer.

Ingredients

2 uncooked salted duck eggs

Chilies (as many as you like), chopped

2 shallots, sliced

2 cloves garlic, sliced

1 green tomato, quartered

2 tablespoons coconut milk

1 tablespoon water

½ teaspoon chicken or mushroom broth powder or bouillon

Salt and pepper, as desired

2 Indonesian bay leaves

4 12x12-inch banana leaves

Instructions

1. Crack one of the eggs into a small bowl.

2. Add the chilies, shallots, garlic, and green tomato.

3. Add the coconut milk, water, broth powder, and salt and pepper.

4. Lay 2 banana leaves on top of each other, one vertical and one horizontal (to avoid leaking, you can put a piece of plastic in between for extra protection). Gently fold one side of the square in so that the center of square forms a cup.

PHOTOGRAPHS COURTESY OF VICTORIA CHRISTINE

5. Put 1 bay leaf in the "cup" and gently pour the raw egg mixture on top. Fold up the banana leaves and secure with a toothpick.

6. Repeat with the remaining egg.

7. Place banana leaf pockets in a preheated steamer pot and steam over low heat for 20 to 30 minutes.

Brown Chicken Stew with Lime (Semur Ayam Jeruk Limau)

Vania Danella (Mount Zion Church, Surabaya)

Ingredients

1 onion, chopped
5 cloves garlic, finely chopped
2 bay leaves
1 whole chicken, cut into 8–10 pieces
2 red chilies, sliced diagonally
1 tomato, quartered
8 tablespoons sweet soy sauce (*kecap manis*)
¼ teaspoon ground nutmeg
Juice of 5 fragrant limes (*jeruk limau*)
1 teaspoon sugar
Salt and pepper, as desired
1–2 potatoes, cut into 4–8 pieces
1 leek, diced

PHOTOGRAPH COURTESY OF
DANIEL TALENTA

Instructions

1. Sauté onion, garlic, and bay leaves with a small amount of cooking oil until aromatic.

2. Add the chicken pieces, cooking until the chicken is browned.

3. Add the chilies, tomato, sweet soy sauce, ground nutmeg, lime juice, sugar, and salt and pepper. Stir to combine.

4. Add water to cover and let it simmer until the chicken is tender.

5. Add the potatoes and simmer until cooked. Add the leek, gently stir. The stew is ready to serve.

Sundanese Liwet Rice (Nasi Liwet Sunda)

Vania Danella (Mount Zion Church, Surabaya)

Ingredients
3 cups rice
6 shallots, sliced
3 cloves garlic, finely minced
1 stalk lemongrass, top trimmed and cut in half
2 bay leaves
3 kaffir lime leaves
2 pandan leaves, knotted together
½ teaspoon salt
½ teaspoon sugar
½ cup coconut milk
2½ cups water
4 bird's eye chilies
4 red chilies, thinly sliced diagonally
2 green chilies, thinly sliced diagonally
10–15 stinky bean seeds (*satawa*; you may omit if desired)
2 tablespoons dried anchovies, fried

Instructions

1. Wash the rice with running water until the water runs clear. Drain and set aside.

2. Preheat 1 tablespoon cooking oil in a large pot. Add shallots and garlic and stir-fry until fragrant. Add lemongrass, bay leaves, kaffir lime leaves, and pandan leaves; stir-fry until fragrant. Add washed and drained rice, salt, and sugar. Stir to mix everything.

3. Pour in the coconut milk and stir again. Transfer to a rice cooker, add water, and cook as you would regular plain white rice.

4. Preheat 1 tablespoon of cooking oil in a skillet. Add bird's eye, red, and green chilies and cook until aromatic. Then add the stinky beans, and cook again.

5. About 5–10 minutes before the rice is cooked, pour the chili mixture and the fried dried anchovies on top of the rice.

6. As soon as the rice is completely cooked, stir to mix everything. Let it rest for another 15 minutes.

7. Serve the warm dish with fresh lettuce, cucumber, tomato, and Indonesian basil on side. You can also add side dishes such as fried chicken, fried tofu, and tempeh.

Omah Laut's "Pindang Serani"

Danang Kristiawan (GITJ Jepara)

Ingredients

1 pound fish (whole or fillets; red snapper, catfish, tuna, or other varieties work well)

7 shallots, thinly sliced

4 cloves garlic, crushed and finely chopped

2 stalks lemongrass, crushed (using mortar and pestle or back of knife)

2 bay leaves

3 lime leaves

1-inch piece fresh ginger, crushed

1-inch piece fresh turmeric, roasted and crushed

1-inch piece fresh Thai ginger (*gangal*), roasted and crushed

Juice of 1 lime

5 red chilies, sliced

1 teaspoon sugar

½ teaspoon pepper

Salt, as desired

2 starfruit (*belimbing wuluh*)

2 tomatoes, roughly sliced

Thai basil, to garnish

Instructions

1. If starting with a whole fish, clean and scale fish. Portion into steaks, wash, and pat dry.

2. Sauté shallots and garlic for 1 minute. Add lemongrass, bay leaves, lime leaves, ginger, turmeric, Thai ginger, and lime juice and stir well. Add 2 cups water and bring to a boil.

3. Add the fish, chilies, sugar, pepper, and salt, stirring well. Add the starfruit and cook for 5 minutes, or until fish is cooked through.

4. Before serving, add the tomato and Thai basil.

Crushed Spicy Chicken (Ayam Geprek)

Ayam geprek is an Indonesian crushed fried chicken with delicious chili paste on top. The chicken is basically crushed upon serving with chili paste toppings. Serve it with salted egg, fresh slices of cucumber, and steamed fried rice on the side for a very delicious Indonesian meal combo.

Fried chicken
½ chicken, divided into big portions
Salt and pepper, as desired
2 eggs, beaten
1 cup flour
Oil for deep-frying

Chili paste
4 red onions, chopped
4 shallots, chopped
4 cloves garlic
6 red chili peppers
13 Thai chilies

Instructions
1. Prepare the chicken for breading, season with salt and pepper. Dip chicken into beaten eggs, let any excess egg drip off, then roll pieces in flour. Repeat for the remaining chicken.

2. Deep-fry chicken in batches until it is golden brown and very crispy.

3. In another pan, deep-fry red onions, shallots, garlic, red chili peppers, and Thai chilies until soft.

4. Using a strainer, strain the onion mixture from the oil. Mash it together, mixing well. (You may use a blender to make it a puree, but most cooks only mash and mix it together.)

5. To serve, smash the crispy chicken with a meat tenderizer (or mallet) and top it with the chili paste. Serve with salted egg, fresh slices of cucumber, and steamed fried rice.

Fried Indonesian Tempeh (Tempeh Goreng)

Tempeh, or tempe, is a traditional Indonesian soy product, similar to tofu, that is made from fermented soybeans. You can just use sugar if you do not have coconut blossom sugar. Use less of the sambal if you do not like spicy foods.

Ingredients
9 ounces tempeh (soybean cake)
¾ cup plus 1½ tablespoon sunflower oil
1 teaspoon grated fresh ginger
1–2 teaspoons sambal (hot sauce)
4 tablespoons sweet soy sauce (*kecap manis*)
1 teaspoon coconut blossom sugar or granulated sugar
Pinch of salt

Instructions
1. Cut the tempeh into thin slices about ¼ inch thick.

2. Heat ¾ cup oil in a deep pot. To check to see if the oil is hot enough, put a small piece of tempeh in the oil. If the oil starts to sizzle and bubble, it is hot enough.

3. Fry the tempeh in batches until they are brown and crunchy. Try approximately 3–4 minutes for each batch at first, and if the tempeh is not yet brown and crunchy, try a few minutes longer.

4. Scoop the tempeh out of the oil with a heat-proof spatula and leave to drain on some paper.

5. Separately, heat 1½ tablespoon oil in another pan. Add the ginger, sambal, sweet soy sauce, sugar, and salt to the pan, mix together, then add the fried tempeh.

6. Fry for a few minutes while you stir regularly. The *kecap manis* mixture will become very sticky and will form a glossy layer around the pieces of tempeh.

7. Scoop the tempeh out of the pan and serve immediately. This tempeh goes well with rice and veggies.

Mixed Vegetables with Peanut Sauce (Gado-Gado)

Gado-gado is a salad, usually flavored with peanut sauce, that has been part of Indonesian cuisine for centuries. There are lots of variations, but it's typically made with vegetables, protein (such as egg, tempeh, and/or tofu), a nutty sauce, and sometimes rice or rice crackers. This recipe uses quinoa.

Ingredients
½ cup white or red quinoa (well rinsed and drained)
1 cup water
1 cup green beans, trimmed
½ medium red bell pepper, thinly sliced
¾ cup mung bean sprouts
⅔ cup thinly shredded red cabbage
2 whole carrots, thinly sliced
Cilantro, as desired
Lime wedges, as desired
Red pepper flakes, as desired

Spicy peanut sauce
⅓ cup salted creamy peanut butter (or substitute almond butter, cashew butter, or sunflower seed butter)
1 tablespoon gluten-free tamari (or soy sauce)

2–3 tablespoons maple syrup, or to taste

3 tablespoons lime juice

1 teaspoon chili garlic sauce, or more to taste (may use 1 Thai red chili, minced; or ¼ teaspoon red pepper flakes)

3–4 tablespoons water (to thin)

Instructions

1. Heat a small saucepan over medium heat and add rinsed, drained quinoa. Toast for 3–4 minutes, stirring frequently, to remove excess liquid and bring a nutty flavor to the quinoa. Then add 1 cup water, stir, and bring to a low boil. Reduce heat to a simmer, cover, and cook for about 18–20 minutes, or until all liquid is absorbed and quinoa is tender. Fluff with a fork, remove lid, and remove from heat.

2. While quinoa is cooking, steam green beans until just tender. You can do this either in the microwave (covered, in 1-minute increments) or by placing green beans in a steamer basket inside a large saucepan filled with 1 inch of water. Bring the water to a simmer on medium-high heat, cover, and cook until just tender—about 4 minutes. Once steamed, add green beans to a bowl of ice water to "shock" them (stop them from cooking). Set aside.

3. Prepare peanut sauce: In a small mixing bowl, combine peanut butter, tamari, maple syrup, lime juice, and chili garlic sauce. Whisk together. Then add water 1 tablespoon at a time, until a semi-thick but pourable sauce is formed.

4. Taste and adjust flavor as needed, adding more tamari for saltiness, lime juice for acidity, maple syrup for sweetness, or chili garlic sauce for heat. You want the sauce to be a balance of tangy, sweet, salty, and spicy, so don't be shy with the seasonings!

5. To serve, divide quinoa between two serving bowls and top with green beans, red bell pepper, mung bean sprouts, red cabbage, and carrots. Serve with peanut sauce and any additional toppings, such as cilantro, lime wedges, and red pepper flakes. Store leftovers separately in the refrigerator up to 4–5 days. Best when fresh.

Pork Satay

Satay (or sate) is a typical Indonesian street food consisting of small pieces of meat grilled on a skewer and served with a spiced sauce that usually contains peanuts. The skewers can also be broiled instead of grilled.

PHOTOGRAPH COURTESY OF DANIEL TALENTA

Ingredients
2 cloves garlic
½ cup chopped green onions
1 tablespoon chopped fresh ginger root

1 cup roasted, salted Spanish peanuts
2 tablespoons lemon juice
2 tablespoons honey
½ cup soy sauce
2 teaspoons crushed coriander seed
1 teaspoon red pepper flakes
½ cup chicken broth
½ cup butter, melted
1½ pounds pork tenderloin, cut into 1-inch cubes

Instructions

1. In a food processor, process garlic, green onions, ginger, peanuts, lemon juice, honey, soy sauce, coriander, and red pepper flakes. Puree until almost smooth. Pour in broth and butter, and mix again.

2. Place pork cubes in a large resealable plastic bag, and pour mixture over meat. Marinate in the refrigerator for 6 hours, or overnight.

3. Preheat grill to medium heat. Remove pork cubes from bag, reserving marinade, and place meat on skewers.

4. In a small saucepan, boil the marinade for 5 minutes. Reserve a small amount of the marinade for basting, and set the remainder aside to serve as a dipping sauce.

5. Lightly oil preheated grill. Grill 10–15 minutes, or until well browned, turning and brushing frequently with cooked marinade. Serve with dipping sauce.

Pineapple Tart Nastar

Chialis Thuan

Pineapple jam
4 cups grated pineapple
¾ cup sugar
½ teaspoon ground cloves
1 teaspoon cinnamon
2 tablespoons butter

Tart dough
1 cup butter
½ cup sugar
2 egg yolks
1½ cup all-purpose flour
¾ cup cornstarch
¾ cup powdered milk

Egg wash
3 egg yolks
2 tablespoons milk
1 tablespoon canola oil

Instructions
1. Prepare the jam filling: Cook the grated pineapple, sugar, cloves, and cinnamon until the pineapple mixture thickens. Add the butter and stir. Remove from heat and allow to cool.

2. Separately, cream together the butter and sugar. Add the egg yolks, mix together. Combine the flour, cornstarch, and powdered milk in a separate bowl, then mix into the butter mixture. Knead thoroughly.

3. Form a 1½-inch ball of dough and flatten into a circle.

4. Fill the flattened dough with a spoonful of pineapple jam, close the dough around the jam, and roll into a ball. Repeated with remaining dough and jam.

5. Bake at 285°F for 30–35 minutes.

6. Whisk together the egg wash ingredients and wash on each tart ball.

7. Bake for an additional 10–15 minutes, or until golden brown.

The Author

John D. Roth is professor of history at Goshen College, editor of *Mennonite Quarterly Review,* and director of the Institute for the Study of Global Anabaptism at Goshen College. He received his PhD from the University of Chicago. Roth's many books include *Choosing Against War: A Christian View*; *Beliefs: Mennonite Faith and Practice*; *Stories: How Mennonites Came to Be*; and *Practices: Mennonite Worship and Witness*. Roth lives in Goshen, Indiana.